Nāgārjuna's *Twelve Gate Treatise*

Studies of Classical India

Volume 5

Nāgārjuna's
Twelve Gate Treatise

*Translated, with Introductory Essays,
Comments, and Notes*

by

Hsueh-li Cheng
*Dept. of Philosophy and Religious Studies,
University of Hawaii at Hilo*

D. Reidel Publishing Company

Dordrecht : Holland / Boston : U.S.A. / London : England

Library of Congress Cataloging in Publication Data

Nāgārjuna, 2nd cent.
  Nāgārjuna's Twelve gate treatise.

  (Studies of classical India ; v. 5)
  Translation of: Dvādaśanikāyaśāstra.
  Bibliography: p.
  Includes indexes.
  1. Mādhyamika (Buddhism)   I. Cheng, Hsueh-li. II. Title. III. Series.
BQ2782.E5C47   1982   294.3'85   82-9858
ISBN 90-277-1380-4   AACR2

Published by D. Reidel Publishing Company,
P.O. Box 17, 3300 AA Dordrecht, Holland

Sold and distributed in the U.S.A. and Canada
by Kluwer Boston Inc.,
190 Old Derby Street, Hingham, MA. 02043, U.S.A.

In all other countries, sold and distributed
by Kluwer Academic Publishers Group,
P.O. Box 322, 3300 AH Dordrecht, Holland
D. Reidel Publishing Company is a member of the Kluwer Group

Printed in the Netherlands

TABLE OF CONTENTS

INTRODUCTION

MĀDHYAMIKA

The hallmark of Mādhyamika philosophy is 'Emptiness', *śūnyatā*. This is not a view of reality. In fact it is emphatically denied that *śūnyatā* is a view of reality. If anybody falls into such an error as to construe emptiness as reality (or as a view, even the right view, of reality), he is only grasping the snake at the wrong end (*Mk*, 24.11)! Nāgārjuna in *Mk*, 24.18, has referred to at least four ways by which the same truth is conveyed:

> Whatever is dependent origination, we call it emptiness. That is (also) dependent conceptualization; that is, to be sure, the Middle Way.

The two terms, *pratītya samutpāda* and *upādāya prajñapti*, which I have translated here as 'dependent origination' and 'dependent conceptualization' need to be explained. The interdependence of everything (and under 'everything' we may include, following the Mādhyamika, all items, ontological concepts, entities, theories, views, theses and even relative truths), i.e., the essential lack of independence of the origin (cf. *utpāda*) of everything proves or shows that everything is essentially devoid of its assumed essence or its independent 'own nature' or its 'self-existence' (cf. *svabhāva*). Besides, our cognition of anything lacks independence in the same way. Our conception (cf. *prajñapti*) of something *a* essentially depends upon something *b*, and so on for everything ad infinitum. Emptiness is thus shown in both ways, from the ontological point of view and from the epistemic point of view. Sometimes, this is expressed in the form of an argument: The truth of everything is emptiness because of the dependent origination of everything. (Compare the introductory comments of Nāgārjuna in

Vigrahavyāvartanī.) The above description, shorn of its awkward technicalities inherited through translation, from the style of the original Sanskrit formulation, can be re-stated for moderners as follows. The Mādhyamika argues that what we might call 'the absolute conception of reality' should be regarded as entirely *empty*. An absolute conception of reality — a reality which all representations represent but is itself independent of them — is what is presupposed by our traditional natural science and also forced upon us by our very conception of Knowledge. Knowledge, understood as distinct from error etc., is presumably knowledge of a reality that may exist independently. It is knowing what is there *anyway*, and what is there anyway is supposed to be unaffected, unmodified, by our knowing it in any particular way. And know we must always in some particular way or other.

Assuming that we wish to combat solipsism or some extreme form of idealism, we may put the point in another way. We seem to have a determinate picture of the world, what it is like, independent of any Knowledge, i.e., any representation of it in thought, any conceptualizations, beliefs, experiences and assumptions. But that picture is ever elusive to us, for we have only different, endless representations of it. No matter how deeply we may think, we may only have another representation of it in thought. It seems that each representation, barring gross absurdities and incoherence, could claim to be 'knowledge', and, what is worse, there is no vantage point from which we have an absolute representation of reality. Our conception of knowledge unfolds the implicit paradox: it projects the conception of an independent reality but also turns it into an ever receding picture — a mirage. No representation can provide finally sufficient substance to that picture. An absolute conception of reality is therefore empty — a 'truth' that dawns upon us as it did, so it is claimed, to the final meditative insight of the Mādhyamikas.

Emptiness or vacuity seems to be at times horrifying, and, to be sure, at times attractive and alluring. The modern man, particularly the Western man, finds this boldness to be rather intriguing and it evokes two very different sorts of response or reaction. There are those who find in such forms of Buddhism an escape route from everything that they need to get away from, dogmas, superstitions, irrational beliefs, faith and even rationality! For emptiness seems to change the very meaning of rationality. Lao Tzu begins *Tao Te Ching* with this verse:[1]

The Way that we can talk about or describe is not the Way.

I am not sure whether the Taoist and the Mādhyamika meant the same thing, but undoubtedly they used very similar language to say what they wanted to say. This contributed to the creation of the Western notion of 'Oriental mysticism' as the take-off point to the realm of irrationality. Those who boast of Western rationality, therefore, find such Buddhism positively repulsive and maddening. It is, they claim, the realm of 'illogic', and there-fore, of insanity. Both of these attitudes towards Mādhyamika philosophy are wrong and misleading. Both of them grab, to repeat Nāgārjuna's own imagery, emptiness at its wrong end. I do not need to repeat Nāgārjuna's cynical warning: Emptiness grabbed at the wrong end is like a snake grabbed at its tail; it is fatal.

The philosophy of emptiness is not a regress into the primordial chaos of irrationality. It is true historically that Mādhyamika supplied the broad philosophical basis for various forms of Bud-dhist practices ranging from pure meditation to exotic Buddhist Tantra rituals for ecstasy. But this will be a subject for historians, not philosophers. What should interest the philosophers today is the fact that Mādhyamika philosophical texts (and the present text is a good specimen) constitute undoubtedly an important component of our global heritage in philosophy. Mādhyamika is a valuable expression of human rationality. This point needs to be stressed in order to counteract the widespread Western misconception to the effect that Mādhyamika is of a piece with the so-called irrational Oriental mysticism. Mādhyamika, for me, is philosophy, i.e., an integral part of what we call today philo-sophic activity. It is akin to the position of radical scepticism

only if a radical sceptic can be said to have a position at all. I do
not see how a radical sceptic can consistently hold to a position
that can be formulated and defended. And the Mādhyamika
will say 'OM' (= Ditto). Nāgārjuna says in *Vigrahavyāvartanī*
(v. 29):

I have no *pratijñā* (= proposition, position) to defend.

Mādhyamika is sceptical of all philosophical doctrines, tenets,
categories. It could be argued that Mādhyamika is therefore not
philosophy, it is anti-philosophical. I consider this argument to
be fallacious. If 'philosophy' is understood to mean broadly
rational discourse on demonstrable answers to some meaningful
questions, Mādhyamika certainly falls into this category. Philosophy is one of the few disciplines which turns to itself. A comparison comes to my mind. It is a comparison with the discipline
called 'natural theology'. Anthony Kenny has recently written
(*The God of the Philosophers*):[2]

... If we take natural theology to be philosophical analysis
of the concepts used in thinking and talking about God, then
a disproof of God's existence, or a demonstration that the
very notion of God was incoherent, would itself be a successful piece of natural theologizing. (p. 4, Oxford, 1979).

The Mādhyamika attempt to show that all philosophical (or
even common-sensical) views of reality are basically incoherent
would, I assert, be also a successful piece of philosophizing in the
same manner.

VITAṆḌĀ

A few words about the nature of the philosophical arguments
used by the Mādhyamikas may be in order here. Their method
of argument belonged undoubtedly to the tradition of philosophic
debate (*vāda* or *vivāda* tradition) that evolved out of the earlier
tradition of sophistry and eristic. In a philosophic debate, the
general strategy is to refute (cf. *dūṣaṇa*) the rival positions, and

establish and defend (*sthāpana*) the philosopher's own position.
A sceptic or a Mādhyamika excelled in the first (*dūṣaṇa*). In fact,
the second was thought by some either unnecessary (e.g., one
might formulate one's own position but not think it necessary to
establish or defend it, cf. the Advaita Vedānta of Śrīharṣa) or
impossible or both (e.g., a true sceptic, or even a Mādhyamika,
in order to be consistent, had to say that he was unable to formulate his position for there was no position he held to). This type of
debate where refutation was the only game that could be played
was called *vitaṇḍā* (cf. *Nyāyasūtra*, 1.2.3).[3]

Vitaṇḍā was obviously used in a pejorative sense as is evident
from the comments of the Naiyāyikas like Vātsyāyana. A debater
who indulged in *vitaṇḍā* was pictured generally as an iconoclast,
who had nothing at stake, or was a motiveless, maligning sort of
person. But this was both incorrect and unfair when we think
of such philosophers as Nāgārjuna, Sañjaya (an agnostic), Jayarāśi
(a sceptic) and Śrīharṣa (a Vedāntin), who restricted their philosophic activity to the 'refutation only' kind of debate (*vitaṇḍā*).
Elsewhere I have shown that the later Nyāya tradition acknowl-
edged this fact and said that the 'refutation only' kind of debate
can also claim philosophical respectability.[4]

PRASAṄGA

The argument-pattern used by the Mādhyamikas as well as other
debaters was called *prasaṅga*. It literally means an implication or
a consequence, but it is used in the technical sense of an argument
that has undesirable and unacceptable implications, or leads to
absurd consequences. In fact, a position (or, a philosophic concept)
is here examined in the light of one or several alternative (and
mutually exclusive) interpretations or formulations and it is
shown that in each case we end up with some absurdity or other.
Hence the position is refuted, for otherwise the argument will
lead to an absurd situation. In this general sense, therefore, we can
call it a *reductio*.

How can one refute all positions? Is it not itself a position:

refutation of all positions? If we say that there is no fact of the matter, is it not another fact of the matter? How can we avoid this obvious paradox? I have discussed elsewhere how a Mādhyamika can avoid the paradox or how a radical form of scepticism can be made consistent.[5] Briefly speaking, a debater can go on refuting all possible, and formulable, positions each at a time and then, when no position is forthcoming, can stop without making the *obvious* claim that all positions have been refuted, for the mere statement of that claim would engender a new position that needs to be refuted again. Obviously we cannot make noise crying out 'Silence!' when all noise-makings have already stopped, for if we did, another shout of 'Silence!' would indeed be needed to silence the first shouting. And then another and another. Nāgārjuna himself uses this analogy of silence and noise-making in his *Vigrahavyāvartanī* (verses 3, 4, 25) to make the same point.

The second point that needs to be made in this connection is that refutation here need not, and should not, be construed as the standard logical negation of a position or proposition. It seems better to view such a refutation as an illocutionary act in the manner suggested by Searle where some illocutionary force is negated rather than a proposition.[6] If this is done, then also the air of paradoxicality involved in the Mādhyamika arguments seems to disappear.

To explain briefly: when a Mādhyamika refutes some position in a debate, it should be construed as what the Sanskrit philosophers call *prasajya pratiṣedha*, or simply *pratiṣedha*. I am now inclined to describe it as an act of illocutionary negation, where the speaker or the person who negates, assumes provisionally (cf. *prasajya*) something to be the case and then 'negates' it or rejects it. This negating act need not commit him to anything else except the rejection of what was assumed to be the case. A distinction between rejection and denial may be understood as follows: denial of something to be the case amounts to assertion of something not being the case, i.e., assertion of the falsity of that case. But rejection is non-assertive in withholding assent to something being the case, and this will then leave it open for us to withhold assent to the same thing not being the case. We may consider Searle's example in this light. "I do not promise to come" does not obviously constitute another 'negative' promise, and hence it is possible to say that I do not promise to come nor do I promise not to come. (In fact, I should say that I do not promise *anything* just as the Mādhyamika says, "I do not assert anything.")

TWO LEVELS OF TRUTH

A Mādhyamika, strictly speaking, is not a radical sceptic, but a Buddhist. Being a Buddhist, he must make a skilful use of the doctrine of the two levels of truth: the conventional or 'concealing' truth and the ultimate truth. For Nāgārjuna himself has warned:

> Those who do not understand the distinction between these two truths, do not understand the deep significance of the Buddha's teaching. (*Mk.* 24.9)

In a way, it can be said that the doctrine of the two levels of truth is implicit in almost every metaphysical inquiry. A philosopher looks for the *reality* behind *appearance*, a doctrine of phenomena is circumscribed by a postulate of noumena, a reductionist tries to reach the *basic* elements out of which the *gross* world has been constructed, an analysis of *physics* makes room for the entrance of *metaphysics*. But the Mādhyamika use of this doctrine of the two levels of truth is very different. The Mādhyamika does not ask us to penetrate through the seeming reality, the appearance, to reach the rock-bottom reality in the usual sense. For there is no rock-bottom reality to begin with (or to arrive at, as the case may be) except what our inherent tendency to misconceive and to misconstrue (cf., *avidyā*) creates for us for the time being. Reality is emptiness, void, vacuity; or, to put the matter differently, the seeming reality or the appearance is all that there is and it is exactly as it is supposed to be, i.e., devoid of any 'own nature', of any essence, any value — it is empty. The 'concealing' reality does not, in fact, conceal anything, or what amounts to the same thing, it conceals EMPTINESS. Therefore, according to the Mādhyamika, the philosophers' search for the ultimate reality must end up in a quagmire of confusion, unless it leads him to Emptiness. To say that emptiness is the ultimate reality is again like the attempt to shout 'Silence' when all noises have already died down and hence it will only destroy silence. If the philosophers are looking for an ultimate reality, besides what is called the Appearance, a reality which is better and more secure than the Appearance, then the truth is that there isn't any such thing. The Appearance is the reality when it is properly understood. The *saṃsāra* is the *nirvāṇa*, says Nāgārjuna (*Mk.* 25.19).[7] This realization of the vacuity, if the Buddha was right, is not, and should not be, horrifying, for it is the very essence of peace, it is bliss, it is *śānta* and *śiva*. It is the cessation of all our discursive thoughts, all misguided drives and misconceived propensities and their attendant frustrations. It is *prapancopaśama*,[8] 'a complete recovery from the malady of manifoldness'.

Professor Hsueh-li Cheng has prepared this annotated translation of the Chinese version of the *Dvādaśa-dvāra* which will unearth further materials of the Mādhyamika philosophy for modern scholars. This will certainly stimulate further research in the history of Indian philosophy. More importantly, this, we hope, will also show the relevance of the study of the Mādhyamika texts in the present-day context. One of the express aims of our series has been to provide annotated translations of important philosophical texts of classical India. We have already presented two such volumes — one on Śrīharṣa and the other on Udayana (see Volumes 1 and 4). The present text is attributed to Nāgārjuna. I am sure the scholarly world in general, and Buddhologists in particular, will welcome this volume.

All Souls College, Oxford   BIMAL KRISHNA MATILAL

NOTES

[1] Wing-tsit Chan, *The Way of Lao Tzu*, New York, 1963.

[2] Anthony Kenny, *The God of the Philosophers*, Oxford, 1979, p. 4.

³ Nyāyasūtra 1.2.3. *sa pratipakṣa-sthāpanā-hīno vitaṇḍā*. Here "*sa*" can refer to, according to Sānātani, either to "*jalpaḥ*" in 1.2.2 or "*vādaḥ*" in 1.2.1.

⁴ B. K. Matilal, *Nyāya-Vaiśeṣika*, Otto Harrassowitz, Wiesbaden, 1977, p. 92.

⁵ B. K. Matilal, *The Logical Illumination of Indian Mysticism*, Oxford, 1977, pp. 10–14, and Notes 12 and 13.

⁶ J. Searle, *Speech-Acts: An Essay in the Philosophy of Language*, Cambridge, 1969, pp. 32–33. My point is further discussed in B. K. Matilal: *Logical and Ethical Issues in Religious Belief*, Calcutta University, 1978, Stephanos Lectures (forthcoming).

⁷ Mr. Cheng, however, does not agree with this comment of mine.

⁸ Nāgārjuna, *Madhyamaka-kārikā* (*Mk.*), Ch. 18, verse 9.

PREFACE

Since the beginning of the twentieth century there has been a growing interest in Buddhism in the West. Many Occidental scholars, philosophers and psychologists are engaging in the study of Buddhist thought, and young people are reading Buddhist literature and practicing meditation. The major purpose of this book is to facilitate understanding of Buddhism, especially of Nāgārjuna's thought, by presenting his *Twelve Gate Treatise* in English translation.

Nāgārjuna lived in the second century A.D. and founded Mādhyamika Buddhism. He is considered one of the greatest thinkers of India and his philosophy is thought of as "the central philosophy of Buddhism"[1]. Scholars have done extensive studies and systematic presentations of Nāgārjuna's writings since early in the century. However, certain aspects of his teachings have not been adequately treated. This is partly due to the fact that some important texts of Mādhyamika Buddhism are still unknown to scholars; one of these is the *Twelve Gate Treatise*. For instance, T. R. V. Murti, a well-known contemporary Mādhyamika scholar, wrote, "Nowhere does the Mādhyamika concern itself directly with issues like god, soul, matter, creation, etc."[2].

But actually, the Mādhyamika does discuss those issues in the *Twelve Gate Treatise*. Nāgārjuna does not explicitly claim that he is a Mahāyāna Buddhist in the *Middle Treatise* or the *Mūlamadhyamikakārikā*, which does not mention the term. This has led some scholars to wonder whether Nāgārjuna is really a Mahāyānist. A. K. Warder once stated,

Modern students have sometimes supposed that he (Nāgārjuna) is criticizing early Buddhism, or the early schools, in order to set up Mahāyāna instead. Is there any truth in this supposition?

1

We have already pointed out that there is nothing overtly Mahāyānist . . . [3].

It seems to me that the problem of whether Nāgārjuna was a Mahāyāna Buddhist would be resolved if one had just read only the first few paragraphs of the *Twelve Gate Treatise*, where Nāgārjuna clearly stated that the treatise was given to expound the essential teachings of Mahāyāna.

In China, Korea and Japan, Nāgārjuna's school of thought is known as the San-lun Tsung (the Three Treatise School) for it is based upon three main texts; namely, the *Middle Treatise*, the *Twelve Gate Treatise* and the *Hundred Treatise*. According to Chinese San-lun masters, one should study these three texts together in order to gain a broad philosophical understanding of Buddhist thought. These works comprise the canonical literature of many other Buddhist schools. Nāgārjuna became the revered patriarch of various Mahāyāna sects. Unfortunately, the *Twelve Gate Treatise*, which is a concise summary of Nāgārjuna's philosophy, exists only in Chinese. This book introduces the *Twelve Gate Treatise* to English readers and presents Mādhyamika teachings from Chinese sources.

In the translation I have attempted to be as close as possible to the original text. However, when the literal Chinese would convey little or no meaning in English, I have expressed the Chinese freely. In Chinese grammar the subject or predicate of a sentence is often understood and therefore not included. So in some instances I have taken the liberty of providing the subject or predicate in the translation for the sake of readability in English. To assist the general reader as well as the specialist in understanding ideas and technical terms, I have given a brief introduction to each chapter and included paragraphs of explanation in the body of Nāgārjuna's arguments; these are labeled *COMMENT*. Words enclosed in brackets are additions not contained in the original. Expressions in parentheses are alternative translations, principally by Sanskrit terms or romanized Chinese characters.

A list of Chinese terms has been provided for those who want to refer to the Chinese originals of certain key terms in the text. The glossary will serve as a brief Buddhist dictionary of important Sanskrit, Pali, Chinese, Japanese and English words used in the book. Throughout the work, the abbreviation "T" is given to indicate the *Taishō Shinshū Daizōkyō*.[4]

I wish to gratefully acknowledge the assistance of faculties of the Center for Buddhist Studies at the University of Wisconsin-Madison, and University of Hawaii at Hilo. A special word of appreciation is due to the late Dr. Richard Robinson, Dr. M. Kiyota and Dr. Martin Huntley for their great help in my research on Buddhist religion and philosophy. I also wish to acknowledge my indebtedness to Dr. Timothy Woo, Dr. Kenneth K. Inada, Dr. Paul McCarthy, John Paxson, Marc Cohen, Walter Westcott, Mrs. Jack Hoes and Judy Graham who read the manuscript and offered suggestions. The encouragement of my colleagues, Dr. Evyn Adams, Dr. Donald Wells and the late Dr. Hideo Aoki has been a powerful stimulus to the completion of this work. A sincere appreciation is extended to Dr. David C. Purcell Jr., Dean of the College of Arts and Sciences, University of Hawaii at Hilo, for providing secretarial assistance in typing and copying the manuscript. I am grateful to Prof. Bimal K. Matilal of Oxford University and Prof. J. Moussaieff Masson of University of Toronto, who reviewed the manuscript at the final stage and gave valuable comments. Special acknowledgement is due the following publishers, for their permission to use certain materials: Cambridge University Press, Fordham University Press, University of Wisconsin Press, and Dialogue Publishing Company. I have used some materials from my own articles in the following journals: 'Nāgārjuna, Kant and Wittgenstein: The San-lun Mādhyamika Exposition of Emptiness', *Religious Studies* (March, 1981), and 'Truth and Logic in San-lun Mādhyamika Buddhism', *International Philosophical Quarterly* (September, 1981). Finally I thank my wife, Alice Chiong-huei Cheng, for her acute criticism, enlightened advice and wholehearted support.

1. NĀGĀRJUNA AND THE SPREAD OF HIS TEACHINGS

It is difficult and even impossible to arrive at a completely accurate, historical account of Nāgārjuna's life because later Buddhists have tended to embellish and fictionalize him. There are often different and conflicting accounts of the life and work of Mādhyamika's founder. Some sources confuse Ārya Nāgārjuna (*Lung-shu: c.* 113–213), the founder of Mādhyamika Buddhism, with Siddha Nāgārjuna who lived some four hundred years later. And two birthplaces, Vidarba and Kāñchi, are given for Nāgārjuna.

Almost all accounts, however, agree that Nāgārjuna was born in South India, came from the Brahman caste and received a Brahmanical education. Also, that he nearly died while still a youth. According to Tibetan sources, astrologers had predicted that Nāgārjuna would die prematurely at the age of seven. His parents believed the astrologers and sent him away because they could not bear to witness his death. This source of tradition alleges that he escaped death by entering the Buddhist order. According to his translator Kumārajīva, Nāgārjuna was overpowered with sensuous desire and passion in his early days. He and three friends entered a royal palace, by making themselves invisible, and seduced its women. But royal guards soon discovered and slew Nāgārjuna's three friends. This experience stirred him deeply and awakened him to the truth that lust is an origin of suffering and misfortune. He vowed to become a *śramaṇa*, a Buddhist monk or ascetic, if he could escape alive. He did escape, entered the Buddhist order and studied all the Buddhist scriptures then available to him. He recited and mastered the Hīnayana Tripiṭaka in ninety days, but was not satisfied and sought further.

Nāgārjuna is said to have obtained the Mahāyāna scriptures from a Nāga (dragon, elephant or serpent) and to have been satisfied with the teachings of the texts. He devoted his life to

4

expounding and propagating the Mahāyāna message. He spent his later days at Bhramaragiri (Śrīparvata) in a monastery built for him by a Śālavāhana King.[1]

Many works have been credited to Nāgārjuna, but it is difficult to know exactly how many are authentic. However, if we accept the *Mūlamadhyamakakārikā* as authentic, we can accept the authenticity of *Dvādaśa-dvāra-śāstra* (the *Twelve Gate Treatise*), *Vigraha-vyāvartanī* and *Yukti-ṣaṣṭika*, for the contents of these are similar and exhibit the essentials of Nāgārjuna's philosophy.[2]

Mādhyamika Buddhism was further developed by Āryadeva (*T'i-p'o: c.* 163–261). He, too, was a native of South India and came from the Brahman caste. Generally speaking, Nāgārjuna used dialectic to attack Hīnayāna Buddhism. Āryadeva believed that Nāgārjuna's dialectic could also be used to refute all other philosophies, and he used it to criticize Brāhmanism. He debated publicly with the Brāhmanists and converted them; he also proselytized a hostile South Indian King.

Āryadeva's main teachings are found in *Catuḥśataka* (*Catuḥ-Śatikā* or simply *Śataka*), his most important work. Although the Sanskrit original has been lost, the text is preserved in its entirety in Tibetan. There are also three different Chinese versions: (1) *Śata-śāstra* (Hundred Treatise), (2) *Śata-śāstra-vaipulya* (Broad Hundred Treatise) and (3) a commentary by Dharmapāla on the *Śata-śāstra-vaipulya*. The *Akṣara-śataka*, falsely attributed to Nāgārjuna in the Tibetan source, is probably the work of Āryadeva. Its Sanskrit original is also lost, but it is preserved in the Chinese. In addition, Āryadeva composed four other works.

After the fifth century, Indian Mādhyamika Buddhism was divided into two schools, the Prāsaṅgika and the Svātantrika. The founder of the Prāsaṅgika School was Buddhapālita and its most eminent philosopher was Candrakīrti (600–650). According to this school, the real and only method of Nāgārjuna and Āryadeva was *prasaṅga* (*reductio ad absurdum*) wherein the true Mādhyamika does not and should not take any position of his own. His chief and sole task is to reduce to contradiction or inconsistency the systems and arguments of opponents proceeding from principles accepted by them. For the Prāsaṅgika, all mental activity produces illusion, and what we call existence is simply a fabrication of images and does not have reality. The real and true language of Buddhist emptiness (*Śūnyatā*) is silence. Candrakīrti wrote several important and authoritative commentaries on Nāgārjuna and Āryadeva's works; of these the *Prasannapadā* is the most valuable. It is a commentary on the *Mūlamadhyamakakārikā* and provides the chief Sanskrit source for the study of Nāgārjuna's philosophy among contemporary scholars.

Bhāvaviveka was the founder of the Svātantrika School. He held that the Buddhist doctrine of emptiness does not assert the non-existence of things but only denies the erroneous assertion of existence. For this school, empirical things are not real from the standpoint of ultimate truth, but have empirical reality. Svātantrika Mādhyamikas criticized Prāsaṅgika Mādhyamikas for engaging in mere negation and refutation without offering a positive viewpoint. They even seemed to hold that it is not necessary to realize *Śūnyatā* in order to enter into *nirvāṇa*.

In expounding their teachings, the Svātantrikas had made certain compromises with earlier Indian Sautrāntika and Yogācāra philosophical thought, and subsequently divided into the Sautrāntika Svātantrika and the Yogācāra Svātantrika. The first school was introduced to China in the seventh century and the second school to Tibet in the eighth century. Yogācāra Svāntantrika Mādhyamika has continued to be the major philosophy in Tibet and Mongolia to this day.

Nāgārjuna's *Middle Treatise* and *Twelve Gate Treatise* and Āryadeva's *Hundred Treatise* have been emphasized by Chinese Mādhyamika Buddhists, devoted to the doctrine of emptiness. So Mādhyamika Buddhism is called the San-lun Tsung (Three Treatise School) in China. The spread of the San-lun School in China began with advent of Kumārajīva (344–413), the most important person in the history of San-lun in China, Korea and Japan. He arrived at Ch'ang-an about 401 where he translated and handed down Nāgārjuna's works and other Buddhist scriptures until his death in 413. It is said that Kumārajīva had three thousand disciples, but most were not intellectuals and did not truly understand Mādhyamika philosophy. Even Kumārajīva complained about the poor quality of his disciples; "If I applied my writing-brush and wrote a Mahāyāna Abhidharma, I would surpass Kātyayanīputra. But now in the land of Ch'in (China) the profoundly intelligent are rare. My wings are broken here, and what would I discourse about?"[3]

Nevertheless, a few students were well educated and made a great contribution to Kumārajīva's work. They helped him translate Buddhist texts and wrote prefaces to the important translations which are invaluable sources for understanding Mādhyamika Buddhism. Kumārajīva's most brilliant disciple seems to have been Seng-chao (374–414), born in the vicinity of Ch'ang-an. Seng-chao grew up in a poor family, but determined to pursue his studies under adversity and received a good education. He wrote several essays and treatises to propagate Buddhism. They show that he had mastered the Mādhyamika theory of knowledge, ontology and philosophy of language. Kumārajīva read the writings and wrote, "My understanding does not differ from yours, and in phrasing we might borrow from each other"[4]. With Seng-chao, Buddhism entered upon a new stage in China. For the first time there was a systematic Buddhist philosophy presented by a Chinese. His philosophical essays helped to root the Mahāyāna philosophy from India in Chinese soil.

Next to Kumārajīva, Chi-tsang (549–623) was the most important Sun-lun master in establishing the San-lun Mādhyamika School and expounding San-lun doctrine. A native of Nanking, he heard about Buddhist teachings while attending lectures by Paramārtha (500–569) and joined the Buddhist order at the age of seven. He received special training for twenty-five years and eventually became an outstanding Chinese commentator as well as one of the great systematizers of Chinese Buddhist philosophy. He worked in the Chia-hsiang Monastary and was known as the Great Master Chia-hsiang. Throughout his career he was highly esteemed and honored by both Sui and T'ang emperors.

Chi-tsang wrote commentaries on the *Middle Treatise*, the

Twelve Gate Treatise, the *Hundred Treatise*, other works by Nāgārjuna and other Buddhist texts. Perhaps his most important book is the *Profound Meaning of Three Treatises (San-lun-hsüan-i)*[5] in which he expounded the doctrine of emptiness as the teaching of *p'o-hsieh-hsien-cheng*. The so-called *p'o-hsieh-hsien-cheng* means that the refutation of erroneous views is the illumination of right views. For Chi-tsang, to see that all things are empty is to understand that all views are erroneous and ought to be rejected. And to refute erroneous views neither implies nor entails that one has to establish or take any view. It simply means the absence of views. The Buddha's teaching of emptiness does not aim to present any view, but to be 'empty' of conceptual speculations. In another important work, the *Meaning of the Twofold Truth*,[6] Chi-tsang examined the nature and function of truth, and pointed out that Nāgārjuna's idea of the Buddhist twofold truth does not stand for two fixed sets of truth nor refer to two realities. It is merely a tactical device used to show that no truth is absolutely true, and thereby to help rid people of dogmatic views.

Chi-tsang presented several reasons for asserting that the *Middle Treatise*, the *Twelve Gate Treatise* and the *Hundred Treatise* should be grouped together for study, and due to him the Chinese San-lun School was firmly established. The San-lun philosophy he presented was authentic Indian Mādhyamika thought. However, the philosophy became too abstract for the Chinese, and consequently the school declined after Chi-tsang died.

Although the San-lun School has not been a sectarian school in China since the eighth century, it has been required as an academic discipline and its teachings have been accepted by many Buddhists throughout East Asia. Nāgārjuna's philosophy has inspired Buddhists to create various philosophical and religious movements. Different Buddhist schools selected certain aspects of Mādhyamika teachings and regarded them as essential, the original teachings of the Buddha, and therefrom developed their own doctrines and religious practices. Some used Nāgārjuna's thought to support an ontological commitment so as to establish a new metaphysics;

this is well illustrated in the formation and development of T'ien-t'ai and Hua-yen Buddhism. Other Buddhists employed Nāgārjuna's teaching to support the view that one has to discard not only intellect but also the entire human effort to obtain salvation; this can be seen in Pure Land Buddhism. Mādhyamika thought has led some Buddhists to embrace nihilism and turned others to mysticism.

Hui-wen (550–577), the founder of T'ien-t'ai Buddhism, attributed his understanding of Buddhism to Nāgārjuna. He is said to have been awakened to the truth by Nāgārjuna's statement, "Emptiness is called the middle way. For it is a provisionary name for the fact that all things are causally dependent upon each other."[7] The verse seems to assert that dependent co-arising (all things are causally related) is synonymous with emptiness (*k'ung*) and the temporary name (*chia-ming*) of the middle way (*chung-tao*). Reading this, Hui-wen at once perceived the triple truth: namely, the truth of emptiness, the truth of temporariness and the truth of mean. For Hui-wen, (1) all things or *dharmas* are empty because they are produced by causal conditions and hence are devoid of self-nature; but (2) they do have temporary existence; and (3) being empty and temporary is the nature of *dharmas* and is the mean. These three — emptiness, temporariness and mean — penetrate one another and are found perfectly harmonized and united. A thing is void but exists temporarily. It is temporary because it is void, and the fact that everything is void and at the same time temporary is the middle truth. One should not consider the three truths as separate but as the perfectly harmonious threefold truth.

According to the T'ien-t'ai School, the three truths are, in reality, three-in-one and one-in-three. The principle is one, but the way of explanation is threefold, and each of the three truths has the value of all. If we argue from the standpoint of emptiness, we may deny the existence of the temporary and the middle, for we consider emptiness as transcending all. The three would be empty. The same will be the case if we argue from the standpoints of temporariness or mean. So when one is empty, all will be empty;

when one is temporary, all will be temporary; when one is middle, all will be middle. They are otherwise called the identical emptiness, identical temporariness and identical mean; and also the absolute threefold truth.[8] Although T'ien-t'ai doctrine may not be a correct interpretation of Nāgārjuna's teaching, it developed out of Mādhyamika thought.

Hua-yen Buddhists developed the somewhat similar one-in-all and all-in-one philosophy. Fa-tsang (643–712), the founder of Hau-yen Buddhism (known as the Kegon School in Japan), was once a Mādhyamika disciple. He seemed to have been fond of the *Twelve Gate Treatise* and wrote a book on it (*Shih-erh-men-lun-tsung-chih-i-chi*). One of the most important messages in his book is that if one thing is empty, all will be empty. Fa-tsang seemed to have been inspired to an idea of a world in which all things are interwoven in perfect harmony by mutual penetration and mutual identification. According to Fa-tsang and his followers, true Buddhism is not merely a criticism of all views, but should aim at establishing a harmonious whole, having the perfectly enlightened Buddha as the essence at the center. Hua-yen Buddhists made an ontological commitment to the Buddha as infinite, all-pervading and omnipresent. Everything in the universe, animate and inanimate, performs the work of the Buddha, and inspired by his spiritual influence, even inanimate things lead us to the state of enlightenment.[9]

While T'ien-t'ai and Hua-yen Buddhists were engaged in establishing certain metaphysical systems, other Buddhists attended to Nāgārjuna's criticism of metaphysics. The Mādhyamika teaching of emptiness as the rejection of speculative theory seemed to suggest that reason, intellect or other human effort could not be used to know the mystery of the world or to find true wisdom and obtain *nirvāṇa*. This laid the foundation for the development of Pure Land Buddhism and the formation of the anti-intellectual, irrational and unconventional teachings and practices in Ch'an (Zen) Buddhism.[10]

Pure Land Buddhists hold that one cannot achieve the goal of *nirvāṇa* by effort, but may attain it by the grace or help of Amita

Buddha. According to these Buddhists, Nāgārjuna discovered the Buddha's 'original' teaching of the Way of Faith. Nāgārjuna is reported to have said, "Although there are innumerable ways in the teachings of the Buddha, they can be classified roughly: the Difficult Way and the Easy Way" [11]. The so-called difficult way is to approach *Avaivartika* (a state of no return to the delusive world) by the practice of the eightfold path or the six *pāramitās* (the six virtues of perfection); the easy way teaches us faith in Amita Buddha. T'an-luan (476—524), a great Pure Land master in China, held that in the *Daśabhumi-vibhāsa-śāstra* Nāgārjuna recommended to us, with poor spiritual capacity, the way of faith. T'an-luan claimed to follow Nāgārjuna when he distinquished between the teachings of self-power (*jiriki* in Japanese) and other-power (*tariki*). The first means "to be a lamp unto yourself"; one achieves personal salvation or enlightenment by oneself. But the second tells us that we are saved by the Buddha's compassion and power, not our own. Although Nāgārjuna's teachings bore only a remote relation to the later popular Pure Land doctrine, he was given the great honor by Shinran (1173—1262), the founder of the Shin sect of Pure Land Buddhism in Japan, of being the First Patriarch in the transmission of Amita Buddha's "Gospel of Pure Grace" [12].

The Mādhyamika teaching that all things are devoid of nature, characteristic and function led other Buddhists to take a nihilistic view. In fact, the San-lun School and the Cheng-shih School, which holds that nothing exists at all, were sometimes treated as the same sect in China and Japan. The *Satyasiddhi*, the main text of Cheng-shih nihilism, was studied along with Mādhyamika works by many of Kumārajīva's disciples and other Buddhists. [13] Nāgārjuna's criticism of realism gave some stimulus to the acceptance of Cheng-shih Buddhism among Chinese and Japanese monks. It also turned Buddhists to mysticism; Mādhyamika emptiness seems to suggest that Dharma or the true state of things has to be known not by discursive reasoning, but through mystical intuition. Mystical Buddhists such as the Chen-yen (known as the Shingon in Japan) attributed their understanding of the Buddha's

teachings to Nāgārjuna and accepted him as their patriarch, one
of the most important links in the transmission of Dharma since
Śākyamuni. Kobo Daishi, the founder of the Shingon School in
Japan, was named after the doctrine of emptiness and called Kukai,
which means literally "the empty ocean".

In view of its importance in Buddhism, Nāgārjuna's thought
can well be reckoned as the foundation of Mahāyāna religion.
One cannot adequately comprehend Buddhist teachings and
practices without at least indirectly knowing his philosophy.

2. SAN-LUN APPROACHES TO EMPTINESS

The word *k'ung* (empty or emptiness), which is the main theme of Nāgārjuna's *Twelve Gate Treatise*, seems to have multiple usages and multiple meanings in Chinese San-lun literature. A variety of implications are well developed in the Chinese master Chi-tsang's *Profound Meaning of Three Treatises* (*San-lan-hsüan-i*) and his *The Meaning of Twofold Truth* (*Erh-ti-i*). Both were a result of years of study of Nāgārjuna's work, including the *Twelve Gate Treatise*.

By itself the term has no definite meaning, but acquires various meanings on different occasions. It is often used by San-lun Buddhists to mean the absence of something. San-lun Buddhists may claim that all things are empty in the sense that things are devoid of definite nature, characteristic and function. As Nāgārjuna wrote in the *Twelve Gate Treatise*,

All things are empty. Why?
Neither created nor non-created things
have characteristics.
Since they have no characteristics
they are empty.[1]

The term *empty* is also used to discount and discredit things or concepts. People tend to employ conceptual schemes to describe the nature of things. To say that all things are empty is to suggest that concepts or categories through which one constructs experience are unintelligible. In arguing, for example, that the reality of things cannot be explained by the interplay of concepts, such as being and non-being, or existence and non-existence, Nāgārjuna claimed, "Again, all things are empty. Why? Being and non-being are neither obtainable at the same time nor at different times."[2]

Empty or *emptiness* is sometimes used to devalue things and to designate weakness. Empty things are worthless and should be discarded. As a result, to realize emptiness is to eliminate disaster, the San-lun master Chi-tsang said. "The essence of the sage's teaching (emptiness) consists in the elimination of disaster."[3]

On occasion, to empty one's mind is to change one's mind.[4] Or emptiness is regarded as a medicine (yao)[5] for "curing the disease of all sentient beings"[6]. Emptiness, according to San-lun masters, is mainly a soteriological device or pedagogic instrument (chiao-ti)[7] – a tool used to help people obtain enlightenment.[8]

The way of emptiness is essentially the way of nirvāṇa, and involves mental, physical, intellectual and spiritual aspects. Religiously, emptiness connotes mokṣa, a total freedom or liberation from ignorance, evil and suffering in this world.[9] Psychologically, emptiness is non-attachment. It requires that emotional and intellectual attachements, which are sources of evil and suffering in life, should be purged. The doctrine of emptiness advocates that one empty the mind of passions and illusions.[10] Ethically, this negation of cravings, especially of egoistic desire, will enable one to love all men equally. Nirvāṇa is for all people.[11] The man of emptiness is the man of karuṇā (compassion), who helps all sentient beings obtain nirvāṇa.[12] Epistemologically, emptiness is prajñā, an unattached insight that no truth is absolutely true. The so-called ultimate truth (chen-ti, paramārtha-satya) and worldly truth (su-ti, saṁvṛti-satya) are relative to each other (hsiang-tai or hsiang-chi).[13] Such wisdom is a positive force in the elimination of extremes and ignorance so that one may be enlightened.[14] Metaphysically, emptiness means that all things are devoid of nature, character and function. It teaches that an ontological entity (or entities) given by metaphysicians is not real in the universe, but a mental fabrication. Metaphysical speculation should be discarded as one seeks nirvāṇa.

For San-lun Buddhists, the doctrine of emptiness suggests a way of life. Ordinary men desire sensual pleasure and often believe it is one of the most valuable things in life. On the other hand, religious persons who love spiritual values may look down upon sensualists and think that the spiritual life has nothing to do with pleasure. For the Mādhyamikas, the hedonistic way of life is one extreme and the ascetic way of life is another. The doctrine of emptiness is given to "empty" a person of these extremes and prepare him to live "the middle way". Hence it is regarded as the same as the doctrine of the middle way (*chung-tao-kuan*). This teaching of emptiness as the middle way, according to San-lun Buddhists, was the Buddha's original teaching. It was expressed in the Buddha's First Sermon [15] to five medicants as follows:

> To devote oneself to ascetic practice with an exhausted body only makes one's mind more confused. It produces not even a worldly knowledge, not to speak of transcending the senses. It is like trying to light a lamp with water; there is no chance of dispelling the darkness . . . .
>
> To indulge in pleasures also is not right; this merely increases one's foolishness, which obstructs the light of wisdom . . . .
>
> I stand above these two extremes, though my heart is kept in the Middle. Sufferings in me have come to an end; having been freed of errors and defilements, I have now attained peace. [16]

For the Mādhyamika, the Buddha's teaching aims at rejecting dualistic thought and feeling. Philosophers may use polar concepts such as origination or extinction, permanence or impermanence, sameness or difference, and arrival or departure, to describe the nature of events. These conceptual views are extreme and should be refuted, Nāgārjuna wrote.

> I salute the Buddha,
> The foremost of all teachers,
> He has taught
> The doctrine of dependent co-arising,
> [The reality of things is marked by]
> No origination, no extinction;

No permanence, no impermanence;
No identity, no difference;
No arrival, no departure.[17]

Nāgārjuna's idea of emptiness as the middle way of eightfold negation (*pa-pu-chung-tao*) does not imply eight negations merely, but the total negation of all extreme views, a process of purifying the mind. Negation has to be employed until intellectual and emotional attachments are eradicated from one's life. This process is dialectical in character. The denial of the concept *is* does not entail the affirmation of the concept *is not*, because the latter is shown to be as contradictory or absurd as the former. Mādhyamika dialectic aims not to establish a thesis, but merely to expose the absurdity or contradiction implied in an opponent's argument. It is purely analytic in nature until there is no position left to be proved. Chi-tsang wrote,

> In order to make this point clear, San-lun doctrine teaches that each thesis that may be proposed concerning the nature of truth must be negated by its antithesis, the whole process advancing step by step until total negation has been achieved. Thus the idea of existence, representing worldly truth, is negated by that of non-existence, representing ultimate truth. In turn the idea of non-existence, which now becomes the worldly truth of a new pair, is negated by the idea of neither existence nor non-existence, and so forth until everything that may be predicated about truth has been negated.[18]

This dialectical method is well illustrated in the Chinese San-lun analysis of the concepts *yu* (Being) and *wu* (Non-being). Philosophers may dispute whether Being or Non-being is the reality of the universe. Metaphysicians may assign what is real or what *is* to the realm of Being, and what is unreal or *is not* to the realm of Non-being. And they may make ontological commitments to Non-being as well as to Being. Nothing or non-being, as the name of something, may be regarded as more real than Being itself. Thus Lao-tzu claimed that "being comes from non-being"[19]. But since San-lun Buddhists contended that all metaphysical views are dogmatic, the concepts of being and non-being are both unintelligible. To say that either Being or Non-being is the reality of the universe, and has priority over the other, is an extreme view. Buddha's Dharma, according to San-lun masters, is given to "empty" the concepts of *is* and *is not*. Nor does this teaching of the middle way (*chung-tao*), for which Mādhyamika is named,[20] imply that reality is beyond Being and Non-being, but, again, that metaphysical or conceptual speculations should be eliminated.

Taking another approach, San-lun Buddhists pointed out that what is real must have its own essential nature, and cannot be dependent upon other things or come from causal conditions. But to claim that anything is ultimately real would contradict the fact that all phenomena are bound by the relations of cause and effect, unity and diversity, and duration and destruction. For the Mādhyamikas, the perceived object, the perceiving subject, and knowledge are mutually interdependent. Whatever we can know through experience is conditioned, so it cannot be ultimately real.[21]

Alternatively, San-lun Buddhists argued that that which is unreal can never come into existence. If it exists, it must have certain characteristics through which we know its existence. But that which is unreal has no characteristics, so it is absurd to say that something is unreal. Therefore Being as something unreal cannot be established. Thus Being cannot be defined or described as real or unreal. Hence it is unintelligible to use Being to explain the true nature of the universe; this view, too, is untenable and should be ruled out.

For San-lun Buddhists, the denial of Being does not, further, entail that Non-being can be used to explain and describe the true nature of the universe. To say that Non-being is real is a contradiction in terms and hence makes no sense. For so-called Non-being is without characteristics, while that which is real has characteristics. So, to say that Non-being is the reality of the universe is the same as saying that that which has no characteristics has characteristics; this is contradictory. So, the assertion of the reality of Non-being is unintelligible and should be refuted.[22]

According to San-lun masters, Non-being cannot be defined or described as unreal either. For that which is unreal can never come into existence and hence cannot be perceived. If it can never be perceived, it cannot be described and defined. If it is indescribable or indefinable, how can it be described or defined as Non-being?

According to Chi-tsang, metaphysical speculation about Being and Non-being is at the root of erroneous or perverted views.[23] It involves an attached way of thinking. When people have an ontological commitment to something (whether Being, Non-being, or other things), they ascribe a determinate or own nature (*svabhāva, ting-hsing* or *tzu-hsing*) to it. The thing is believed to possess an essence or quality of being itself.[24]

For Chi-tsang, this attached way of thinking is a kind of disease (*ping*),[25] which leads people to objectify various concepts of the world and multiply realities or ontological entities beyond necessity. Unfortunately, San-lun Buddhists argued, people fail to see this and continue to make ontological commitments to things and become attached to them.[26] Early scholastic Buddhist philosophy, according to Nāgārjuna and his followers, was a good example of this.

For the early scholastic Buddhists, it was erroneous to affirm the reality of absolute Being, *ātman*. But it was not erroneous to affirm the reality of momentary beings, *dharmas* (*fa*). The real, according to them, is not permanent, universal and unitary, but momentary, particular and multiple. The world is composed of an unceasing flow of particular momentary entities. Those entities are the constitutents of our experience and are the truly real events in the universe. Each *dharma* exists for only an instant,[27] and yet is self-sufficient and possesses its own mark or characteristic, which defines its essential nature as different from all others. For example, consciousness is the state of "being aware', and ignorance, of 'lack of cognition'. Though distinct and separated from one another, the *dharmas* are linked together according to the principle of causation. They are not supported or attached to any substance or self.[28]

The Mādhyamikas countered that although it was correct for early scholastic Buddhists to repudiate the concept of *ātman*, they suffered from the same disease as Hindu philosophers: both had made an ontological commitment to something and became attached to it (or them). For the Mādhyamikas, the concept of *dharmas* is as unintelligible as that of *ātman*. They argued that the claim, "*dharmas* exist", is a contradictory or absurd statement. To prove this, they examined the meaning of *existence*, observing that "to exist" means "to be caused", "to be conditioned", "to be produced", or "to be dependent on something".[29] But a *dharma*, as an ontological entity, is by definition a thing which has essential or own nature (*svabhāva*).[30] The so-called own nature is something which is independent and which makes an object what it is and not something else. Therefore to say that a *dharma* exists would be the same as saying that a thing which is independent of everything else is dependent on something. This is a contradiction in terms and hence makes no sense.[31]

According to the Mādhyamikas, other ontological entities can be refuted in a similar way. They are only human concepts and one should not be attached to them. However, philosophers continue to manufacture entities and realities, and project them onto the world. For the Mādhyamikas, this metaphysical speculation is a disease, and the cure of the disease lies not so much in developing a new metaphysical theory as in understanding the nature and function of conceptualization and language. Nāgārjuna claimed that the very language men create and use plays tricks on them and destroys their "eyes of wisdom"[32]. Enlightened men should discard conceptualization so as to avoid being taken in. Emptiness, for San-lun masters, is a medicine for curing the "philosophical disease"[33]

One of the chief sources of confusion in philosophical reasoning, San-lun Buddhists contended, is that philosophers often fail to see the emptiness of words and names. People tend to think that words, names and concepts are attached to objects and belong to them inherently. They believe that words name or denote objects, and that sentences are combinations of such names. Meaning is the thing for which a word stands. If the word does not denote an ordinary object, it may stand for a transcendental or non-empirical entity, and if one knows something, there must be "something" which one knows. Men tend to look for a real object for a word, a real distinction behind a linguistic distinction, a real essence for a linguistic class, a true reality for knowledge. Thus they are led unsuspectingly into metaphysical dilemmas of their own making. Philosophers indulge in metaphysical disputes about questions such as: What is the true state of the universe? Is it Being or Non-being? Is Being one or many? Is it permanent or impermanent? Does Non-being stand for something? Does it have priority over Being? Such metaphysical questions seem genuine, and the chief task of philosophy is to answer them.

According to San-lun masters, Buddha's Dharma is an awareness that metaphysicians have intellectual attachment. They are misled by human concepts and fail to see that metaphysical questions are not genuine. So-called orthodox Buddhist philosophy is, for the San-lun, just another dogmatic view. It does not eliminate metaphysical speculation but merely shifts position from a monistic view (Being is one) to a pluralistic view (Being is many). So the same kind of metaphysical concerns repeatedly occur. For Nāgārjuna and his San-lun followers, one cannot solve the problem by presenting a new metaphysical theory. The complete solution lies rather in taking all metaphysical problems as conceptual confusion without explaining the initial metaphysical mistake by another metaphysical theory. In his critique of all views, Nāgārjuna wrote, "I have no view"[34].

According to San-lun masters, the refutation of erroneous views (p'o-hsieh) is the same as the illumination of right views (hsien-cheng). This means that a critique of a view does not aim to present another view but simply to discard the view. Nāgārjuna's dialectic is not merely to limit the validity of intellect and logic; it is also to declare that reasoning and conceptual speculation are absurd. According to this idea of emptiness as "no view", to look for *prajñā* (wisdom) is not to look for something, but rather to know that "something" is empty. Wisdom is not the attainment of a theory but an absence of it. No truth is "really true"[35].

In expounding on this, Nāgārjuna and his San-lun followers analyzed the nature of language and pointed out that the meaning of a term does not lie in an objective or extra-linguistic entity to which that term corresponds, but lies in the context. If the context changes, the meaning of the word changes or even disappears. In the strict sense, meaning is not part of an object or thing itself, but a human projection. Those who insist that there must be some extra-linguistic reality or essence to which words refer, are "like a man who, perceiving the body of a woman created by magic as really existent, feels desire for her"[36].

When men have the attached way of thinking, they make ontological commitments to truth and falsity as well as to ontological entities. According to Chi-tsang, one should also eliminate attachments to right and wrong, true and false, or affirmation and negation. For him, so-called right and wrong, true and false are equally empty; they do not stand for any essence or self-existing thing. The "right" view is not a view in itself but merely an absence of views. A right view is called "right" because all views have been abandoned. If it were accepted as a view, it would become a wrong view which ought to be rejected.[37]

As we have seen, in San-lun philosophy the illumination of right views and the refutation of erroneous views are not two separate things. Thus, when the Buddha denied that a *dharma* is existent, he did not hold another view that a *dharma* is non-existent. If someone were to hold that a *dharma* is non-existent, this view would be another extreme to be refuted. Although the Buddha sometimes used the word *non-existence* in his dialogues, one should know that "the idea of non-existence is brought out primarily to handle the disease of the concept of existence. If that disease disappears, then useless medicine is also discarded"[38]. Chi-tsang further said, "Originally there was nothing to affirm and there is not now anything to negate"[39].

San-lun masters maintained that no truth is absolutely true.[40]

Every true claim which is so, is so for a particular observer or is made from a particular standpoint. Its truth value is not purely objective. In the strict sense, all truths are conventional; they are human projections. Our minds are often deluded by all sorts of illusions, prejudices and attachments. The truth value of the statements we make, according to the Mādhyamika, lies in whether they involve attachment or not. Those which involve attachment or make men clinging are called *su-ti* (worldly, relative or low truth), and those which do not involve attachment or make men non-clinging, are *chen-ti* (ultimate, transcendent or high truth). However, if ultimate truth is regarded as something fixed or standing for an absolute or self-existing thing, it becomes a new attachment and worldly truth. One has to re-examine it from yet another, higher standpoint and see that all truths are empty.

Ultimately, to realize this empty nature of truth is *prajñā*. True wisdom is knowing nothing substantial. In a strict sense, it has no knowing or knowledge. *Prajñā* is an insight that the act of knowing, the knower, the object to be known, the distinction between the subject and the object, truth and falsity, are all empty. This is a wisdom without attachment; it is synonymous with *Śūnyatā*. This no-knowing and empty nature of *prajñā* is well stated by Seng-chao:

> Thus in *prajñā* there is nothing that is known, and nothing that is seen . . . . It is evident that there is a markless knowing and unknowing illumination . . . . Real *prajñā* is as pure as empty space, without knowing, without seeing, without acting, and without objects. Thus knowledge is in itself without knowing, and does not depend on anything in order to be without knowing.[41]

Unfortunately, the doctrine of emptiness in Mādhyamika Buddhism is often interpreted as absolutism or nihilism; the word *empty* or *emptiness* is regarded as a descriptive name referring to Absolute Being or Absolute Non-being.[42] Actually, the San-lun Buddhist teaching of emptiness as the middle way is the denial of both extremes. The claim that all things are empty means that all things are neither absolutely existent nor absolutely non-existent. This point was succinctly drawn by Seng-chao as follows:

> For what reason? If you would say that [things] exist, their existence arises non-absolutely. If you would say that they do not exist, their forms have taken shape. Since they have forms and shapes, they cannot be the same as "inexistent". So, this explains the idea of the emptiness of the non-absolute.[43]

If the existence of a thing were absolutely real, it would then be self-existent and independent of causes and conditions. But all things are dependent on causes and conditions. So a thing cannot be self-existent and absolutely real. On the other hand, if the universe were non-existent and absolutely nothing, it would be motionless and its phenomena would not arise. But we see that myriad things do arise from various causes and conditions, so they cannot be absolutely unreal. Thus the doctrine of emptiness in San-lun Mādhyamika thought is a middle way, and should not be identified with absolutism or with nihilism.[44]

Actually, the word *k'ung*, emptiness, according to San-lun Buddhists, is merely "a convenient means to lead sentient beings and to enable them to be free from various attachments"[45]. This tool has multiple functions and uses. The Buddha was considered by San-lun masters to be a soteriologist at heart and his teaching to be practical in character. His main concern was the *nirvāṇa* of mankind from evil and suffering, and his teachings were *upāya*, skillful means, used to achieve this goal. The Buddha found that the minds of ordinary people were always attached and bound to views, difficult to emancipate from birth, old age, suffering and death. He intended to help them gain enlightenment, yet he realized that they could understand only mundane things and ordinary language. In order to save them, he used common words, such as cause and effect, existence and non-existence, right and wrong, affirmation and denial, and empty and not-empty, to explain his teachings. In fact, all the words used are nothing more than tools to aid in purifying the mind.

Though language may play tricks on us, the Mādhyamikas do

not deny its practical value. They acknowledge that language is useful and even necessary in daily life, for without language we could neither speak nor write. According to Nāgārjuna, ultimate truth has to be explained by speech, and speech is conventional and conditional. Language as worldly truth is essential for the attainment of ultimate truth and *nirvāna*. Nāgārjuna wrote, "Without worldly truth, ultimate truth cannot be obtained. Without obtaining ultimate truth, *nirvāna* cannot be obtained."[46]

In order to communicate with others, we need conceptualization and predication. The mistake lies in identifying meaning with object, and concept with reality. To avoid this, one should know that words and names are empty. When our words are not regarded as standing for any essence or self-existing object, they can be used to expose the absurd implications of metaphysical speculations. The function of language can be likened to a raft. A man intending to cross a river to get to the other bank, where it is safe and secure, makes a raft. With its help he safely reaches the other shore. But however useful the raft may have been, he will now leave it aside and go his way without it. So also language, including the term *Dharma*, is like the raft, to be discarded after *nirvāna*.

Clinging to or longing for things or ideas is also likened by San-lun Buddhists to fire, and as such a source of suffering, delusion and ignorance. In this analogy, emptiness as a soteriological device becomes like water. But the analogy is complex. Chi-tsang wrote,

> If water could extinguish fire and then again produce fire, what would we use to extinguish it? The view that things come to an end or are eternal is the fire and emptiness can extinguish it. But if one still clings to emptiness, then there is no medicine that can eliminate the disease.[47]

One who knows the proper nature and function of the word *emptiness* and other terms can nevertheless use these concepts to resolve philosophical confusion. Chi-tsang himself used the terms *being* and *non-being*, to clear away a problem in his teaching of Twofold Truth on three levels (*san-tsung-erh-ti* or *erh-ti-san-kuan*).[48]

Ordinary people usually believe that the universe is real and what appears to them through the senses is considered true. They affirm the reality of appearances and hold that they belong to the realm of being (*yu*). But saints or enlightened men, Chi-tsang pointed out, would not accept this realism, and would realize instead that all things are empty. What appears to us through the senses belongs to the realm of non-being (*wu*) rather than being. Realism is treated by Chi-tsang as worldly truth (*yu-wei-su-ti*) and the denial of it as ultimate truth (*wu-wei-chen-ti*). This is the first level of spiritual growth.

On this level, one may be attached to the concept of being. This attachment can be eliminated by knowing that the true state of things is more like non-being than being. However, men may still have an attached way of thinking. Now they make a distinction between being and non-being and hold that the terms *being* and *non-being* are descriptive names standing for two completely different states of affairs. The denial of being is believed to entail the affirmation of non-being. This dualistic way or reasoning is an attachment, a kind of worldly truth (*yu-wu-erh-wei-su-ti*). To know that both being and non-being are empty is ultimate truth (*fei-yu-fei-wu-pu-erh-wei-chen-ti*). This second level of spiritual growth lets people realize that the true state of the universe cannot be described as being or non-being.

But men continue to long for something. They may think that if reality is neither being nor non-being, it must be something beyond being and non-being. For Chi-tsang, this monistic absolutism is another extreme view to be refuted, for that which is beyond being and non-being is really empty. Like the previous, dualistic ways of thinking, this metaphysical viewpoint belongs to worldly truth (*erh-yü-pu-erh-wei-su-ti*). The denial of both dualistic and non-dualistic metaphysics is ultimate truth (*fei-erh-fei-pu-erh-wei-chen-ti*).[49]

Chi-tsang's critical examination of the problem of being and non-being is a means of purifying the mind from various attachments. *K'ung*, emptiness, is used whenever extreme views occur. It has different connotations and implications on various levels. On the first level, emptiness means that common-sense things are illusory and unreal. It is expressed by Chi-tsang as the denial of being. On the second level, emptiness implies that the nihilistic as well as common-sense views of the universe are unacceptable and that all discriminations or dualistic ways of thinking should be dismissed. On the third level, emptiness displays that monistic as well as the dualistic and pluralistic views of the universe should be rejected. It is expressed as the denial of both duality and non-duality. When all conceptualizations and other attachments are completely eliminated, emptiness means "absolutely non-abiding", clinging to nothing.

Thus the word *k'ung* has no meaning by itself, but acquires a meaning in context. It gains its true connotation only in process. When *nirvāṇa* is achieved, it loses its meaning and should be discarded. As with medicine, emptiness is of use to a man only so long as he is ill, but not when he is well again. Chi-tsang said,

> Originally, it was to counter the disease of [belief in] Being that we preached Non-being. If the disease of [belief in] Being vanishes, the Medicine of Emptiness is also useless. Thus we know that the way of the sage has never held to either Being or Non-being. What obstacle can there be, then?[50]

3. THE NATURE AND VALUE OF THE TEXT

Nāgārjuna's *Twelve Gate Treatise* was a principle document in the San-lun tradition for centuries and was also accepted as canonical literature by many other schools. But because it exists only in Chinese translation, modern Western scholars have seldom studied the *Twelve Gate Treatise*. Recently a few have questioned the authenticity of the three treatises, and doubted if they are Nāgārjuna's and Āryadeva's work.[1]

Contemporary Mādhyamika scholars accept the *Prasannapadā* of Candrakīrti as the authentic *Mūlamadhyamakakārikā* of Nāgārjuna. It seems that if the *Prasannapadā* is genuine, then the *Middle Treatise* is also authentic, because the two are almost identical. Since both the main verses and commentaries of the *Twelve Gate Treatise* resemble the main verses of the *Middle Treatise* in their philosophical reasoning, religious assertion and literary style, the *Twelve Gate Treatise* is most likely an authentic Nāgārjuna book.

The *Middle Treatise* was written before the *Twelve Gate Treatise*, as can be seen by the fact that the *Middle Treatise* is mentioned several times in the *Twelve Gate*. In examining the issues of being and non-being, the *Twelve Gate Treatise* states, "This has been discussed in the *Middle Treatise*";[2] and in analyzing the notion of a maker, the *Twelve Gate Treatise* mentions, "As it has been written in the *Middle Treatise* ... "[3] Now, since the *Middle Treatise* was written first and the two works are similar, one may ask why Nāgārjuna wrote the *Twelve Gate Treatise* at all. Why did San-lun masters insist that one should study the book? Several purposes and reasons can be offered.

(1) The *Twelve Gate Treatise* provides a concise account of Nāgārjuna's thought. In a sense it is a simple crystallization of his main teachings in the *Middle Treatise*.

(2) The *Middle Treatise* was written primarily for Hīnayāna

Buddhists, while the *Twelve Gate Treatise* was presented for non-Buddhists as well as Buddhists.

(3) The *Twelve Gate Treatise* discusses certain important religious and philosophical issues which the *Middle Treatise* does not touch on.

(4) The *Twelve Gate Treatise* clarifies certain problems which the *Middle Treatise* does not explain clearly.

Nāgārjuna's *Mūlamadhyamakakārikā* has 27 chapters and consists of 445 verses, or 449 verses in the *Prasannapadā* version. It seems to have been too much for ordinary laymen and even many professional monks to study. In order to make Buddhism easier to understand, a brief but comprehensive presentation of Buddhist thought was needed. The *Twelve Gate Treatise*, which has only 26 verses, seems to have fit the need. Nāgārjuna opened the book with these words:

> Now I shall briefly explain the teachings of Mahāyānism . . . .

> *Question*: Mahāyāna teachings are too many to be counted. Even the sayings of the Buddha alone cannot be exhausted. How can you explain and expound them [all]?

> *Answer*: Because of this, I said at the beginning [this would be] a brief explanation.[4]

In expounding the doctrine of emptiness, the *Middle Treatise* discusses eight negations or the eightfold negation of the middle way; namely, "no origination, no extinction; no permanence, no impermanence; no identity, no differentiation; no coming, no departure"[5]. But the *Twelve Gate Treatise* chooses the first negation and concentrates its argument on the concept of origination or production (*sheng*). Instead of spending time examining the other seven negations, the entire treatise aims at showing that "all things have no production: therefore all things are ultimately empty and tranquil"[6].

The presentation of Buddhist thought in the *Twelve Gate Treatise* is simple and yet comprehensive enough to lead people to know the central message of Buddhism. So Nāgārjuna told readers, "To explain emptiness and enter into its meaning one should use the *Twelve Gate*"[7]. It seems that if one studies the *Twelve Gate Treatise* first, it is easier to understand Mādhyamika teachings in the other treatises. Perhaps this is why Kumārajīva translated the *Twelve Gate Treatise* into Chinese first, then the *Middle Treatise*.

Although both treatises argue for the doctrine of emptiness, the aim of Nāgārjuna's criticism in the *Middle Treatise* is mainly to refute Hīnayāna philosophy, and to this end it examines in detail the concepts of the six sense faculties (*liu-ching*), five *skandhas* (*wu-yin*), six *dhātus* (*liu-chung*) and passions (*jan-jan-che*). The aim of the criticism in the *Twelve Gate Treatise* is to refute both *anātman* and *ātman* traditions. It tries to achieve this goal by analyzing the concepts of nature (*hsing*), mark (*hsiang*) and function (*yung*), and demonstrating that all things, whether *ātman* or *anātman* (substance or elements, are devoid of nature, mark and function. Unlike the *Middle Treatise*, the *Twelve Gate Treatise* devotes comparatively little effort to a discussion of Hīnayāna issues, such as the *skandhas, dhātus* and passions, but it deals with common mistakes of Hīnayāna and non-Buddhist philosophies.

According to the Mādhyamika, a central mistake made by Buddhist and non-Buddhist metaphysicians is that they fail to see that nature, mark and function cannot be established, and hence falsely assert the reality or existence of things. The Mādhyamika argues that if people know that nature, mark and function cannot be established, they will not make ontological commitments. The reasoning is quite simple. For a thing to be real or to exist, it must have a certain nature, mark or function. The Mādhyamika shows that nature, mark and function cannot be established. Thus, for the Mādhyamika, to know that nature, mark and function are empty is the same as knowing that all things are empty. This is one of the main points brought out in the *Twelve Gate Treatise*.

As Nāgārjuna examined the concepts of nature, mark and function in the *Twelve Gate Treatise*, he also discussed certain important religious and philosophical issues which he did not examine in other works. One of these issues is the problem of the existence of God. Nāgārjuna not only ruled out God's existence as the creator of the universe, but also repudiated the concept of God as the savior of mankind. Religious men often think of God as a savior; our fate, destiny and happiness are controlled by Him. If we surrender to Him, He will redeem us from sin and give us happiness. Without God's grace salvation is impossible. Nāgārjuna attacked these ideas and argued that we have certain "self-making powers" such as controlling our passions and behavior so as to produce good and avoid evil.[8] If salvation is only from God, it would destroy "the principle of the world", namely, that men do good and obtain reward, and do evil and receive punishment.[9] One would not need to be mindful, for good deeds might not produce good reward, while evil could bring about salvation. Since this is absurd, salvation cannot be dependent upon God's grace. If God is the sole source of salvation, religious discipline would be of no use. Yet this is not the case, and therefore God cannot be the sole source of salvation.

Another important issue discussed in the *Twelve Gate Treatise* is whether the principle of causality can be proved empirically. People usually believe it can, and the uniformity of causal law is considered an inductive inference. We observe a constant conjunction of causes and effects that justifies the principle that similar causes produce similar effects. However, Nāgārjuna argued that the principle of causality cannot be proved empirically. The constant conjunction of events in the past does not guarantee that similar events will produce similar effects unless we *assume* that similar causes produce similar effects. The empirical justification of the causal principle is really based upon the very principle which we attempt to prove.[10]

Sometimes Nāgārjuna did not present his viewpoint clearly in the *Middle Treatise*, and scholars have been perplexed about his position. For instance, in Chapter XXVI of the *Middle Treatise* he described the twelve chains of causal conditions:

All sentient beings are deluded by ignorance and hence have caused three kinds of action.[11]

Since various actions arise, [the sentient beings] go through six forms of life.[12]

Since it is conditioned by various kinds of action, the consciousness establishes itself with respect to six forms of life.

Since consciousness is established, name and form are instilled.

Since name and form are instilled, the six sense faculties arise.[13]

Through a combination of objects, qualities and discernments, six touches (or perceptions) evolve.

Since six touches evolve, three feelings arise.[14]

Since three feelings arise, desire is produced.

Through desire are four clingings [15] produced, and through the clinging perceptions being is generated.

If the perceiver has no clinging perception, he will be freed and there will be no being.

From being birth arises, and from birth old age and death arise.

From old age and death, misery, grief, despair, and disturbance arise.

These various things arise from birth.

So owing to the twelve chains of causal conditions, great sufferings are produced.

The so-called wheel of life and death is the source of all actions.

The ignorant creates it, but the wise does not.

By the cessation of each component, each subsequent link will not arise.

The accumulation of sufferings is thus completely extinguished.[16]

The teaching is quite different from the message in the previous 25 chapters of the *Middle Treatise*, and has the appearance of Hīnayāna thought. Kenneth K. Inada, who has translated the *Mūlamadhyamakakārikā*, comments upon the chapter:

> In this chapter and the final one to follow, Nāgārjuna goes into the analysis of Hīnayānistic doctrines. The present chapter discusses the twelvefold causal analysis which is the basis of the endless process of suffering incurred by all living beings. The discussion is Hīnayānistic and it reveals that the source of trouble lies in ignorance which in turn initiates all kinds of mental conformations (*saṃskāra*) .... The discussion of the doctrine of causal analysis indicates the strong influence of Hīnayānistic or Abhidharmic teachings during this period.[17]

The teaching here has puzzled many scholars: how do we interpret it? What was Nāgārjuna's real view concerning the twelve chains of causal conditions? Did he become a Hīnayānist at the end of writing the *Middle Treatise*? It seems that these questions can be solved by study of the *Twelve Gate Treatise* where Nāgārjuna clearly presented his view of the twelve chains of causal conditions in the first chapter, and demonstrated that the twelve chains cannot be conceived as the causal law of the world. He used a scriptural passage from the *Seventy Treatise* to introduce his standpoint: "[Twelve chains of] causal conditions really have no production. If they have production, do they have it in one mind-moment or in many mind-moments?"[18]

Nāgārjuna argued that if the twelve chains of causal conditions are the real causal law of the world, they must happen or be produced (a) in one mind-moment, or (b) in many mind-moments.

But one cannot say that all twelve causal factors appear in one mind-moment, for if they occur in one mind-moment, then causes and effects would happen at the same time. This is impossible because a cause must be prior to an effect. Nor can one say that the twelve appear in many mind-moments, for if they occur in different mind-moments, they would be distinct and have no particular relation to each other. Each would occur with a particular mind-moment, then disappear with that mind-moment. If so, how can any of them be a causal condition? Thus, both cases (a) and (b) cannot be established, and hence the twelve chains of causal conditions cannot be conceived as the real internal causal law: they are empty. Nāgārjuna's definitive view is presented in the *Twelve Gate Treatise*. This explains in part why the *Twelve Gate Treatise* is valuable for knowing Mādhyamika thought and also why San-lun masters insisted that one should study the book.

Recently some scholars question whether Nāgārjuna was really a Mahāyāna Buddhist and whether he had ever read the *Prajñāpāramitā sūtras*. For the *Middle Treatise* does not mention the words "Mahāyāna" and "Prajñāpāramitā sūtra". A. K. Warder argues,

> The doctrine of the Buddha, according to Nāgārjuna, consists essentially of the Four Truths and Conditioned Origination. There are no terms peculiar to the Mahāyāna. There is no evidence that Nāgārjuna had ever seen any *Prajñāpāramitā* text − For him the most important canonical text is the *Nidāna Saṁyukta* − Modern students have sometimes supposed that he is criticizing early Buddhism, or the early schools, in order to set up Mahāyāna instead. Is there any truth in this supposition? We have already pointed out that there is nothing overtly Mahāyānist in the *M K (Mūlamadhyamakakārikā)*. Even in its deeper implications there seems to be nothing distinctively Mahāyānist in this reading of the *Nidāna Saṁyukta*. It is not early Buddhism which is being attacked . . . [19].

One who reads the *Twelve Gate Treatise* will have cause to dispute this thesis; the opening statement clears away our doubts. The text describes itself as a concise summary of Mahāyāna teachings, and Nāgārjuna begins with seven reasons why Mahāyāna is superior to Hīnayāna, each of them a discussion of the word *great*, as in,

> This is the vehicle which is ridden by Buddhas and great men, and hence is called great . . . . Again, in the *Prajñā-sūtra*, the Buddha himself says that the teachings of Mahāyāna are immeasurable and boundless. For this reason it is called great.[20]

If one studies the *Twelve Great Treatise* and the *Middle Treatise* together, it becomes clear that the logic in Nāgārjuna's writing is not purely formal. When Nāgārjuna argued, he did not adhere rigidly to form. The four expressions he used are not entirely devoid of logical meaning, yet the meaning of each expression depends on context. Nāgārjuna often viewed each lemma in several different ways. This is especially the case with the third and fourth lemmas.

According to Richard Robinson, the third lemma is a conjunction of the I and O forms of Aristotelian logic. However, a careful study of the *Twelve Gate Treatise* and the *Middle Treatise* shows that Nāgārjuna viewed the third lemma in at least three different ways, namely $(p \cdot \sim p)$, $(p V \sim p)$ and $(I \cdot O)$. Nāgārjuna's arguments sometimes suggest that he regarded or used the third lemma not as a conjunction of I and O, but of p and $\sim p$. In his critical analysis, Nāgārjuna often argued that the lemma itself involves mutually conflicting theses (*hsiang-wei*) and hence is not possible. This is clearly stated in the *Twelve Gate Treatise* when he examined the third possible view of causation:

> It is also untenable that a cause can both include and exclude an effect and then produce the effect. Why? Because including and excluding are contradictory in nature. How can things which are contradictory in nature be together? Just as brightness and darkness, suffering and pleasure, going and staying, binding and loosening cannot be together, so a cause which both includes and excludes an effect cannot produce.[21]

The *Middle Treatise* also suggests this view: "For, how could

the mutually conflicting 'being' and 'non-being' co-exist as one?"
(*yu-wu hsiang-wei ku, i-ch'u tse wu-erh*).[22] In talking about the
third lemma in connection with *nirvāṇa*, Nāgārjuna likewise viewed
it as of the $(p \cdot \sim p)$ form and said, "How could *nirvāṇa* be [in
the realm of] both existence and non-existence? Both cannot
be together in one place just as the situation is with light and
darkness."[23]

On other occasions, Nāgārjuna seemed to treat the third lemma
as a disjunctive affirmation $(p \lor \sim p)$. He did not say that the third
lemma is self-contradictory, but that it may have two fallacies
(*erh-kuo*). For example, in examining the third alternative view of
suffering, Nāgārjuna wrote, "Nor can it (suffering) be made by
both itself and another, for this involves two fallacies ... the
fallacy of self-made and a fallacy of other-made"[24]. If either
of them ('self-made' and 'other-made') can be established, then a
third alternative can be established: "If suffering could be made
individually by itself and by other, then there should also be
suffering made jointly"[25]. Since neither of them can be established: "In truth then, suffering could not be made by itself for a
thing could not make itself. Neither could it be made by other for
the other is insubstantial."[26] So the third alternative cannot be
established. As Robinson suggestes, Nāgārjuna did sometimes
use the third lemma as a conjunction of particular statements
$(I \cdot O)$. In discussing the third alternative view of the relation between man and god, Nāgārjuna interpreted "both eternal and
non-eternal" as "one part is divine and one part is human"[27].

Perhaps one reason why Robinson and other scholars[28] insist
that the third lemma is of the $(I \cdot O)$ form exclusively is that it is
more plausible than the $(p \cdot \sim p)$ or $(p \lor -p)$ forms. For Nāgārjuna,
however, it does not make any difference which logical form is
used to describe reality. All theories about reality, no matter
what their logical forms are, are erroneous, and none can be
claimed more plausible than others. He aimed to show absurdity
in each of them.

It seems that Nāgārjuna also viewed and treated the fourth
lemma in several different ways. He sometimes spoke of it as the

contrary or negation of the third. For example, in discussing the third alternative view of *nirvāṇa*, he wrote that *nirvāṇa* is characterized by both being and non-being (*yu wu*), and in disputing upon the fourth alternative view, declared that *nirvāṇa* is not characterized by both being and non-being (*fei-yu fei-wu*) [29]. However, Nāgārjuna also seems to have treated the fourth lemma as the contrary or opposite of the first three lemmas together. For instance, in arguing upon the first three lemmas of suffering, he stated that suffering "has cause" (is caused by itself, by other, or by both); and in discussing the fourth lemma, he claimed that suffering "has no cause" (*wu-yin*). [30]

The conciseness of the *Twelve Gate Treatise* made it of real use to San-lun masters in China and their pupils. From its pages one gathers that Nāgārjuna may be definitively placed among Mahāyāna Buddhists, and there is, further, the remarkable dispensing with cause and effect, a standard Buddhist tenet. The text is abbreviated, focusing on but one, rather than all eight, of the Buddhist eightfold negations. It shows a flexibility of logical forms, when read in conjunction with the *Middle Treatise*, that makes it of interest to specialists in that area. These are all aspects of the importance of the text.

NOTES

PREFACE

1 T. R. V. Murti says, "Considering the role and the importance of the Mādhyamika, I have ventured to appraise it as the Central Philosophy of Buddhism". *The Central Philosophy of Buddhism* (Allen and Unwin, London 1970), p. vii. M. Hiriyanna says, "In one sense it (the Mādhyamika) is the most important outcome of Buddha's teaching". *Outlines of Indian Philosophy* (Allen and Unwin, London, 1932), p. 206.

2 T. R. V. Murti, 'Samṛti and Paramārtha in Mādhyamika and Advarta Vedānta', in *The Problem of Two Truths in Buddhism and Vedānta*, ed. by Mervyn Sprung (D. Reidel, Boston, 1973), p. 13.

3 A. K. Warder, 'Is Nāgārjuna a Mahāyānist?', *Ibid.*, pp. 80—81.

4 The *Taishō Shinshū Daizokyō* is the Chinese *Tripiṭaka* in 100 volumes, ed. by Junjiro Takakusu and Kaiyoku Watanabe (Daizō Shuppan Company, Tokyo, 1922—34).

1. NĀGĀRJUNA AND THE SPREAD OF HIS TEACHINGS

1 For a detailed life of Nāgārjuna, see M. Walleser's *The Life of Nāgārjuna from Tibetan and Chinese Sources*, Hirth Anniversary Volume, trans. by A. A. Probsthain, ed. by B. Schindler (London, 1922), pp. 421—55. See also K. Venkata Ramanan, *Nāgārjuna's Philosophy as Presented in The Mahā-Prajñāpāramitā-Śāstra* (Varanasi, India, 1971), pp. 25—30, 336.

2 For the work of Nāgārjuna, see K. Venkata Ramanan, *Ibid*, pp. 34—37. See also T. R. V. Murti, *The Central Philosophy of Buddhism*, pp. 88—91; Richard Robinson, *Early Mādhyamika in India and China* (University of Wisconsin Press, Madison, Wisconsin, 1967), pp. 26—27.

3 *Kao-seng-chuan* (T 2509). P. 332; see Richard Robinson, *Ibid.*, p. 96.

4 *Kao-seng-chuan*, p. 365.

5 T 1852 in Vol. 45.

6 *Erh-ti-i*: T 1854 in Vol. 45.

7 *Middle Treatise*, XXIV: 18.

8 See Junjiro Takakusu, *The Essentials of Buddhist Philosophy*, ed. by W. T. Chan and Charles A. Moore (University of Hawaii Press, Honolulu, 1974), pp. 126–137.

9 For Hua-yen thought, see Junjiro Takakusu, pp. 108–125. See also Garma C. C. Chang, *The Buddhist Teaching of Totality* (Pennsylvania State University Press, University Park, 1974).

10 For the influence of Mādhyamika philosophy upon Zen, see Hsueh-li Cheng, 'Zen and San-lun Mādhyamika Thought: Exploring the Theoretical Foundation of Zen Teachings and Practices', *Religious Studies* **15** (1979), 343–363.

11 Ryukyo Fujimoto, *An Outline of the Triple Sutra of Shin Buddhism* (Honpa Hongwanji Press, Kyoto, 1955), I, p. 34.

12 *Ibid.*, pp. 28, 34, 41; see also Alfred Bloom, *Shinran's Gospel of Pure Grace* (University of Arizona Press, Tucson, Arizona, 1968), pp. 7–8, 47, 64.

13 See Junjiro Takakusu, *Essentials*, pp. 74–77. See also Tang Yung-tung, *Han Wei Liang-chi Na-pei Ch'ao Fo-chiao-shih* (Shanghai, 1938), chs. 10, 11.

2. SAN-LUN APPROACHES TO EMPTINESS

1 *Twelve Gate Treatise*, IV: 1.

2 *Ibid.*, VII.

3 Chi-tsang, *The Profound Meaning of Three Treatises* (*San-lun-hsüan-i*, T 1852), p. 1a.

4 Chi-tsang, *The Meaning of the Twofold Truth* (*Erh-ti-i*, T 1854), pp. 79c, 80a, 99b, and 107a.

5 Chi-tsang. *Three Treatises*, p. 91c.

6 Chi-tsang, *Twofold Truth*, p. 91a. See also *Profound Meaning*, pp. 94 and 114.

7 *Twofold Truth*, pp. 78b, 88–90 and 114b. *Three Treatises*, pp. 4c and 7.

8 *Twofold Truth*, pp. 89c and 93b.

9 *Ibid.*, pp. 79c and 80c.

10 Chi-tsang, *Three Treatises*, pp. 1a, 5a, 6a, 7–8, 11b, 12 and 13.

11 Chi-tsang, *Twofold Truth*, p. 22.

12 Chi-tsang, *Three Treatises*, p. 1.

13 Chi-tsang, *Twofold Truth*, pp. 79c, 98c, 101c and 102.

14 *Ibid.*, p. 79b.

15 See Shōson Miyamoto, 'The Buddha's First Sermon and the Original Patterns of the Middle Way', *Indogaku Bukkyōgaku Kenkyū*, XIII, 2 (1965), pp. 855–845, and *Chūdo shisō oyobi sono hattatsu* (Middle Way Thought and Its Development) (Hōzōkan, Kyoto, 1944).

16 Wm. Theodore de Bary, *The Buddhist Tradition in India, China* and *Japan* (The Modern Library, New York, 1969) p. 71; it was translated from the *Buddhacarita*, Sanskrit text ed. by E. H. Johnson (Baptist Mission Press, Calcutta, 1935), pp. 140–142.

17 This is the opening statement of the *Middle Treatise*.

18 Chi-tsang, *Three Treatises*, p. 6.

19 Lao-tzu, *Tao-te-ching*, 40. See *The Way of Lao Tzu*, tr. by Wing-tsit Chan (Bobbs-Merrill, New York 1963), p. 173.

20 The name 'Mādhyamika' was derived from the Sanskrit noun *madhyama*, meaning 'the middle', and the suffix *ka*. The San-lun Tsung in China, Korea and Japan is known as Chung-tao Tsung (School of the Middle Way) as well as K'ung Tsung (School of Emptiness).

21 Chi-tsang, *Twofold Truth*, pp. 82c, 83b, 87a, 88a, 95b, 99b, 102c,

105c and 110; *Three Treatises*, pp. 8a and 10a; *A Commentary on the Middle Treatise*, pp. 112–113.

22 Chi-tsang, *A Commentary on the Middle Treatise*, p. 29.

23 *Ibid.*, pp. 111b and 113a.

24 Nāgārjuna attacked the early scholastic Sarvāstivāda for adhering to self-nature of the *dharmas*. Chi-tsang accepts Nāgārjuna's criticism of Abhidharma philosophy and extends the idea of *svabhāva* to cover all ontological entities which may be used by philosophers.

25 Chi-tsang, *Three Treatises*, pp. 5a, 6, 10c and 11a; *Twofold Truth*, pp. 82, 87a, 91a, 94, 108c and 114b; *A Commentary on the Middle Treatise*, pp. 111–113.

26 *A Commentary on the Middle Treatise*, p. 113a; *Twofold Truth*, p. 91c.

27 Buddhist schools such as the Ābhidharmakośa, the Mahāsanghika, the Mahiśaska and the Sautrāntika hold that only the present is real. But the Sarvāstivadas maintain that the past, the present and the future are real.

28 See Edward Conze, *Buddhist Thought in India* (University of Michigan Press, Ann Arbor, 1967), pp. 34–36 and 92–106.

29 According to the Buddha's teaching of *pratītyasamutpāda*, whatever is existent is caused or conditioned. In the *Middle Treatise* XV: 6–7 and 10–11, Nāgārjuna argued against the static notions of existence and even non-existence. He said, "Those who see the concepts of existence and non-existence [in terms of] self-nature and other-nature, do not perceive the true meaning of the Buddha's teaching" (verse 6). Chi-tsang, *Three Treatises*, p. 8a; *Twofold Truth*, p. 95b; *A Commentary on The Middle Treatise*, pp. 112–113.

30 For a discussion of the word *svabhāva* or own nature, see Richard H. Robinson, *The Buddhist Religion* (Dickenson Publishing Company, Inc., Belmont, Calif., 1970), pp. 51–52.

31 *Middle Treatise* XV: 1–2.

32 *Middle Treatise* XXII: 15. See Chi-tsang, *A Commentary on the Middle Treatise*, pp. 139b, 141a, 144a.

33 *Shang-mei hsi-lun*. Chi-tsang, *Ibid.*, pp. 128 and 139. Chi-tsang, *Three Treatises*, pp. 10c and 11a; *Twofold Truth*, pp. 82a, c, 108c and 114b.

34 See the *Twelve Gate Treatise*, VI, and *Hui-cheng-lun*, 63, 64.

35 Chi-tsang, *Twofold Truth*, p. 97.

36 *Hui-cheng-lun*, 27.

37 Chi-tsang, *Three Treatises*, pp. 7, 14.

38 *Ibid.*, pp. 6, 11.

39 *Ibid.*

40 Chi-tsang, *Twofold Truth*, p. 98.

41 Seng-chao, *Chao-lun*, Part III in T 1858, p. 153.

42 H. Kern, La Vallée Poussin, Max Walleser, A. B. Keith and Harsh interpreted the Mādhyamika teaching of emptiness as the philosophy of Non-being or nothing (nihilism), while T. R. V. Murti, Th. Stcherbatsky, Edward J. Thomas, P. F. Casey, H. N. Chatterjee and S. Radhakrishnan regarded the term *emptiness* as referring to absolute Being or reality (absolutism).

43 Seng-chao, *op. cit*, Part II, p. 152c.

44 For a detailed discussion of this, see Hsueh-li Cheng, 'Nāgārjuna's Approach to The Problem of the Existence of God', *Religious Studies* 12 (1976), 207–216.

45 Chi-tsang, *Three Treatises*, p. 7. This quotation was taken from Chapter One of the *Lotus Scripture* (*Śaddharmapuṇḍarīka sūtra*).

46 *Middle Treatise*, XXIV: 10. See also *Twelve Gate Treatise*, VIII.

47 Chi-tsang, *Twofold Truth*, p. 111.

48 *Ibid.*

49 *Ibid.*, p. 91.

50 *Ibid.*, p. 11. For a detailed discussion of San-lun exposition of emptiness,

see Hsueh-li Cheng, 'Nāgārjuna, Kant and Wittgenstein: The San-lun Mādhya-mika Exposition of Emptiness', *Religious Studies* 17 (1981), 67—85.

3. THE NATURE AND VALUE OF THE TEXT

1 Richard A. Gard, 'On the Authenticity of the *Pai-lun* and the *Shih-erh-men-lun*', *Indogaku Bukkyōgaku Kenkyū* II (1954), 751—742; 'On the Authenticity of the *Chung-lun*', *Indogaku Bukkyōgaku Kenkyū* III (1954), 376—370.

2 *Twelve Gate Treatise*, VII.

3 *Ibid.*, X.

4 *Twelve Gate Treatise*, I.

5 The opening statement of the *Middle Treatise*.

6 *Twelve Gate Treatise*, XII.

7 *Ibid.*, I.

8 *Twelve Gate Treatise*, X.

9 *Ibid.*

10 *Twelve Gate Treatise*, II.

11 "Actions" here refers to dispositions which affect *karma*. The three kinds of action are related to the body, speech and mind.

12 The six forms of life are: hellish things, hungry ghosts, beasts, evil spirits, human beings and heavenly beings.

13 The six sense faculties are eye, ear, nose, tongue, body and mind.

14 The three feelings are pain, pleasure and freedom from both.

15 The four clingings are the clingings of passions, dogmatic views, rigid rules of conduct and selfhood.

16 *Middle Treatise*, XXVI: 1—14.

17 Kenneth K. Inada, *Nāgārjuna: Translation of His Mūlamadhyamaka-kārikā with an Introductory Essay* (Hokuseido Press, Tokyo, 1970), p. 160.

18 *Twelve Gate Treatise*, I: 2.

19 A. K. Warder, 'Is Nāgārjuna a Mahāyānist?', *The Problem of Two Truths in Buddhism and Vedānta*, ed. by Mervyn Sprung, pp. 80–81.

20 *Twelve Gate Treatise*, I.

21 *Twelve Gate Treatise*, II.

22 *Middle Treatise*, VIII: 7.

23 *Ibid.*, XXV: 14.

24 *Twelve Gate Treatise*, X.

25 *Middle Treatise*, XII: 9a.

26 *Ibid.*, XII: 8.

27 *Ibid.*, XXVII: 17.

28 See K. N. Jayatilleke, 'The Logic of Four Alternatives', *Philosophy East and West* (Jan., 1967), Vols. 16–17.

29 *Middle Treatise*, XXV: 15–16.

30 *Ibid.*, XII: 9; *Twelve Gate Treatise*, X. For a detailed discussion of Nāgārjuna's logic, see Hsueh-li Cheng, 'Truth and Logic in San-lun Mādhyamika Buddhism', *International Philosophical Quarterly*, No. 21, September, 1981.

NĀGĀRJUNA'S *TWELVE GATE TREATISE*

TABLE OF CONTENTS [SENG-JUI]

I. CAUSAL CONDITIONS [1]

In the inquiry for the causes of things, it seems that every-thing possesses a nature of itself.[2] A careful analysis shows that such a self-nature does not really exist.
The word "Gate" means a way leading to a thorough under-standing without a residue of doubt.

II. WITH OR WITHOUT EFFECT

This is a further examination of the principle of voidness of self-nature. It begins with the question whether things have been already in existence or have not been in existence prior to their production. Neither alternative is possible to establish the process of production.
This examination constitutes one of the "Gates".

III. CONDITIONS

One previous chapter examines causes and this one examines conditions. Effects cannot be found either in conditions in general or in any one of the four conditions.[3]
This examination constitutes one of the "Gates".

IV. CHARACTERISTICS [4]

The previous three Gates show that production does not exist in the examination of causes and conditions. This one shows that production does not exist in the examination of the three characteristics.[5]
This examination constitutes one of the "Gates".

47

V.   WITH OR WITHOUT CHARACTERISTICS

This examines the reality of the three characteristics: whether they characterize an object with or without characteristics. It shows that there can be no characterization in either case.
This constitutes one of the "Gates".

VI.   IDENTITY OR DIFFERENCE

The issue of the reality and unreality of characteristics have been examined, [Nāgārjuna studies] whether an object and characteristics are identical or different from each other.[6]
Neither case can be established.
This constitutes one of the "Gates".

VII.   BEING OR NON-BEING

The previous chapters show that the three characteristics cannot really characterize; this one shows that the four characteristics[7] cannot, either. "Origination" and "duration" belong to "Being", while "decay" and "destruction" belong to "Non-Being". "Being" and "Non-Being" cannot exist either together or separately.
This constitutes one of the "Gates".

VIII.   NATURE

The examination of Being and Non-Being shows that things are always changing in nature. Since things are originated from conditions, there cannot be any self-nature.
This constitutes one of the "Gates".

IX.   CAUSE AND EFFECT

Things can neither be found from their "self-nature", nor

can be found from the process of causation.
This constitutes one of the "Gates".

X.   THE CREATOR

There cannot be creation without cause and effect. In the examination of four alternative cases,[8] there cannot be any creation.
This constitutes one of the "Gates".

XI.   THE THREE TIMES [9]

In the exhaustive study of creation, it is necessary to examine it with respect to time. Then one will find that creation is impossible in all three times.
This constitutes one of the "Gates".

XII.   PRODUCTION [10]

"Creation" means that something new is formed; "Production" means that something new is originated. Since they cannot be established in all three times, how can there be such a thing as production?
This constitutes one of the "Gates".

PREFACE [SĒNG-JUI]

The *Twelve Gate Treatise* is a refutative and corrective[1] exposition on the nature of reality[2] and the essential way to the place of enlightenment.[3]

Twelve is the great number which comprises all branches [of teachings on emptiness]. *Gate* is the term for opening up, clearing the way and removing hindrances. *Treatise* is the complete examination of sources and the thorough exposition of principles.[4] If one principle is not thoroughly explained, many different views will arise and the point will be missed.[5] If one source is not completely examined, many people will go astray and become heterodox.

If heterodox views are not corrected, and the erroneous not eliminated, great men will be grieved. Therefore Nāgārjuna Bodhisattva opened a way for those who want a solution and wrote the *Twelve Gate* to set them right. By using the *Twelve Gate*, the issue of being and non-being is cleared away, and no [other] problem remains.[6] Once the issue of being and non-being is solved, the problem of God as the creator disappears. When principles culminate in the empty position, the self is lost along with the two extremes. However, losing the self requires the discard of the fishtrap (language).[7] Discarding the fishtrap requires leaving behind reliance [on the doctrine of emptiness].[8] Only when the fishtrap and the self are both forgotten can one comprehend reality. When one comprehends reality, the real and the unreal both disappear, and possessing and losing vanish. Once these disappear and vanish, one can remove hazards[9] in the double mystery[10] [of the doctrine of emptiness], eliminate all erroneous views,[11] turn the carriage toward the place of enlightenment and set the mind fully on the Buddha-stage.

How glorious [is the *Twelve Gate Treatise*]![12] Truly, it is like

51

brandishing an empty blade in an empty space, playing inaudible music in the cosmos,[13] saving the drowned with a profound ford and going beyond the boundary of being and non-being.

How fortunate the scholars of later times! A level road is already prepared, and a hidden pass is already disclosed. Truly, they can ride a gentle phoenix in the Northern Ocean,[14] drive a white ox back to the south, be awakened from the dream state, attain a hundred transformations and turn homeward in peace. As when the bright sun shines forth, there is no dark place that is not illuminated when this is understood.[15]

I, Seng-jui, not very talented, still dare to clarify and verify the empty gate. I long to realize the ultimate ideal, and hope there may be benefits in daily life, and expect there will be good effects in coming years. Moreover, how greatly I respect such talented work. [So] I dare to use my poor pen and limited thoughts to write a preface and add a table of contents at the front. I have done so not because it can increase the value [of the treatise],[16] simply with the hope that I may open a way to improve myself.

I. CAUSAL CONDITIONS

This chapter is divided into two parts. The first part is the preface of the treatise. It states the main theme of the book. The second part is devoted to the examination of the concept of 因緣 (yin-yüan). The word yin (hetu) means cause or reason. It often refers to primary cause. The term yüan (pratyaya) means conditions, cause, relationship by fate or margin. It often refers to secondary cause. For example, a seed is yin, while rain, wind, sun, farmer, etc. are yüan. But in this chapter yin and yüan seem to be used together. Yin-yüan here means causal condition, causal relation, conditioning cause, or causality.

Causality has been an important issue in Indian philosophy. The principle of causality is often regarded by Buddhists as well as non-Buddhists [1] as the objective law regulating the rise and fall of all factors or phenomena in the universe. There are four external causal conditions (外因緣 wai-yin-yüan) and twelve internal causal contions (內因緣, nei-yin-yüan) which are enumerated in early Buddhist treatises. Each of them is conditioned (paṭiccasamuppanna) as well as conditioning (paṭiccasamuppāda). When viewed from the antecedent cause, each is an effect, but when viewed from its effect, it is a cause. [2] The twelve chains of causal conditions are considered as the true picture of the wheel of existence. In this chapter Nāgārjuna argues that all causal conditions are empty.

Nāgārjuna says: Now I shall briefly explain the teachings [3] of Mahāyāna.

Question: What are the benefits of explaining Mahāyāna?

Answer: Mahāyāna is the profound *dharma*-store [4] of the buddhas in the ten directions of space [5] and the three periods of time. [6] It is spoken for the people of great virtue and intelligence. [7] [But] the sentient beings of late times are hardly virtuous and talented. Although they seek [and study] the *sūtras*, they cannot understand. [8] I sympathize with these people and want to enlighten them. [9] And also I want to reveal and make clear the supremely

53

great teachings of the Tathāgata.[10] Therefore, I will briefly explain
the teachings of Mahāyāna.

Question: Mahāyāna teachings are too many [11] to be counted.
Even the sayings of the Buddha alone cannot be exhausted. How
can you explain and expound them [all]?

Answer: Because of this, I said at the beginning [this would be]
a brief explanation.

Question: Why is it called Mahāyāna?

Answer: Mahāyāna is the superior of the two vehicles,[12] and
hence is called the Great Vehicle. This vehicle can [help people]
reach the ideal of the buddhas, and hence is called great. This is
the vehicle which is ridden by buddhas and great men,[13] and hence
is called great. It can eliminate the great sufferings of sentient beings
and give great benefits, and hence is called great. It is the vehicle
ridden by great persons such as bodhisattvas Avalokiteśvara,[14]
Mahāsthāmaprāpta,[15] Mañjuśrī[16] and Maitreya,[17] and hence is
called great. This vehicle can exhaust the bottom of all truths and
hence is called great. Again, in the *Prajñā-sūtra*, the Buddha himself says that the teachings of Mahāyāna are immeasurable and
boundless. For this reason it is called great.

One of the profoundest teachings of Mahāyāna is called empti-
ness. If one can understand this doctrine, he can understand
Mahāyāna and possess the six *pāramitās* [18] without hindrance.
Therefore, I want only to explain emptiness. To explain emptiness
and enter into its meaning one should use the *Twelve Gate*
[*Treatise*].

COMMENT: This statement concludes the preface of the book. The
following is the main body of Chapter I.

The first gate is concerned with causal conditions. It is said,

Things are produced from various conditions,
and hence have no self-nature.
If they have no self-nature,
how can there be such things?

COMMENT: The whole treatise includes twenty-six verses. This is the first verse.

Self-nature (*tzu-hsing, svabhāva*) is the key concept Nāgārjuna wants to refute. He is against the ontologization of any entity or object. A similar issue is examined in 1: 2, 13 and 15: 1–4 in the *Middle Treatise*. Emptiness here means "without self-nature" or "without own essence".

All things produced by various conditions are of two kinds, one internal and the other external. All conditions are also of two kinds, one internal and the other external. External causal conditions are, for example, clay, turning string and a craftsman; together they produce a jar. As another example, a rug is produced from the causal conditions of yarn, a loom and a weaver. Similarly, site preparation, foundation, poles, wood, mud, grass and labor are examples of external causal conditions; together they produce a house. Still other examples are milk, a curdling vat and labor; they are combined to produce cheese. Again, seed, earth, water, sunshine, wind, air, seasons and labor are combined to produce the sprout. One should know that the so-called external causal conditions are all like these. The so-called internal causal conditions are ignorance, action, consciousness, name-form, the six sense faculties, touch, feeling, desire, clinging, formation of being, birth and old age, death; each has a cause first and then is produced.

Thus both internal and external things are produced by various conditions. Since they are produced by various conditions, is it not true that they have no self-nature?

Now if a thing has no self-nature, it cannot have other-nature nor both self-nature and other-nature. Why? Because the so-called other-nature has, in fact, no self-nature.[19] If we say that something exists because of other-nature, then a cow exists because of horse nature; a horse exists because of cow nature; a peach exists because of apple nature; an apple exists because of peach nature, and so on. [They are all] really impossible. One might say that something exists not because of a certain other-nature, but because of a certain other. But this cannot be the case either. Why? If one says that a mat exists because of a certain grass, then the grass and the mat would be one body, and the grass could not be called other. If one says that the grass is other with respect to the mat, then he could not claim that the mat exists because of the grass. Moreover, the so-called grass has no self-nature either. Why? Because the grass is also produced from various conditions. Since grass has no self-nature, one cannot say that because of grass nature the mat exists. Therefore, the mat cannot have grass as its substance. Thus, for the same reason the production of a jar, cheese and other things from external causal conditions cannot be established.

Similarly, production by internal causal conditions cannot be established. As it is stated in the *Seventy Treatise*,

[Twelve chains of] causal conditions really have no production. If they have production,
do they have it in one mind-moment or in many mind-moments?

The so-called twelve causal conditions really and originally have no production. If there is production, does it occur in one mind-moment or in many mind-moments? If it occurs in one-moment, then a cause and an effect would happen together at the same time. But this is impossible. Why? Because a cause is prior to an effect. If production occurs in many mind-moments, then the twelve causal conditions would be distinct from one another. Each of the earlier ones would occur within a particular mind-moment and disappear with that mind-moment. Then, what would be the causal condition of the later ones? Since what disappears with a particular mind-moment is non-existent, how can it affect others? If there are twelve causal conditions, they should either be in one mind-moment or in many mind-moments. But neither is possible.

COMMENT: Nāgārjuna here discusses an idea which is not well examined in the *Middle Treatise* 24: 1—14. He wants to show that the so-called twelve chains of causal conditions are really empty. He also argues that one cannot use mind, consciousness or an internal element to explain the reality of the universe.

Therefore, all conditions are empty. Since conditions are empty, things produced by conditions are also empty. Thus, one should know all created things [20] are empty. If created things are empty, how much more so with the self? [21] Because of created things such as the five *skandhas*, the twelve sense fields (*āyatana*) and the eighteen elements (*dhātu*), one can say there is the self. Only if there is something burnable can there be the fact of burning. Now since *skandhas*, sense fields and elements are empty, nothing can be called self. If there is nothing burnable, there cannot be the fact of burning.

> *COMMENT*: Buddhists divide existence into two main groups, *saṁskṛta* and *asaṁskṛta*. The *saṁskṛta* comprise such *dharmas* as are tied to chains of causation and are capable of producing effects, while the *asaṁskṛta* exist unconditionally. The five *skandhas*, twelve sense fields and eighteen elements belong to the *saṁskṛta*. Space, *nirvāna* and a negative state due to the absence of proper conditions belong to the *asaṁskṛta*.
>
> The five *skandhas* are form (*rūpa*), sensation (*vedanā*), perception (*sanjñā*), impulse (*saṁskāra*) and consciousness (*vijñāna*). The twelve sense fields (*āyatana*) are the eye, objects of sight, the ear, sounds, the nose, smells, the tongue, tastes, body, touchable objects, mind and mind-objects. The eighteen elements are the six sense faculties, the six sense objects and the corresponding six sense consciousnesses.
>
> Nāgārjuna argues that both the *saṁskṛta* and the *asaṁskṛta* are empty. Since they are empty, all things are empty.

The *sūtra* says, "The Buddha told *bhikṣus* [22] that because of self there can be self belongings. If there is no self, then there are no self belongings." [23]

Thus, since created things are empty, we should know that the non-created *nirvāna* is also empty. Why? The elimination of the five *skandhas* without producing another five *skandhas* is called *nirvāna*. [But] the five *skandhas* are originally empty. What is to be eliminated to be called *nirvāna*? And the self is also empty. Who can obtain *nirvāna*? Moreover, non-produced things are called *nirvāna*. If produced things can be established, non-produced things can be established. As mentioned in the previous examination of causes and conditions, produced things cannot be established. This will be discussed again. So produced things cannot be established. Because there are produced things, others can be called non-produced. If produced things cannot be established, how can non-produced things be established?

Therefore created things, non-created things and the self are all empty.

II. WITH OR WITHOUT EFFECT

This is the longest chapter in the treatise. Nāgārjuna examines here the relationship between cause and effect to show that causal relation cannot be explained rationally. If there is a causal relation, is cause with effect and then produces it? Or is the cause first without the effect and then produces it? Nāgārjuna argues that neither case can be established. The issue is also whether an effect is already real in a cause or at the outset unreal in a cause, and whether an effect pre-exists in a cause or not. Nāgārjuna tries to point out that causal production is impossible by showing that causal relation cannot be established.

Nāgārjuna uses the logic of the tetralemma to discuss the issue. There are four possible views of causality, namely (1) an effect is already real in a cause, (2) an effect is at the outset unreal in a cause, (3) an effect is both real and unreal in a cause, and (4) an effect is neither real nor unreal in a cause. His analysis is concentrated on the first two cases.

Again, things are not produced. Why?

> If an effect is already real [in a cause],
>   there can be no production.
> If at the outset unreal [in a cause],
>   there can be no production either.
> If both real and unreal,
>   there can be no production.
> How can there be production?

If an effect is already real in a cause, then there will be no production. If an effect is at the outset unreal, there will not be production either. If an effect is both real and unreal, there will be no production either. Why?

If an effect is already real in a cause and becomes [again] a product, there will be an infinite regress. If an effect is that which is not yet produced and becomes a product, then that which is already produced should have a product again. Why? Because they are originally real in a cause. Even the effect of that which is already produced should have production again. So there will be an infinite regress.

If it is said that that which is already produced can never be produced again, but that which is not yet produced can be produced, there is no principle of production [in the situation]. Therefore, it is impossible that an effect is already real in a cause and becomes a product.

> COMMENT: Nāgārjuna seems to say that since an effect is already real, both *wei-sheng* (the production which is not yet produced) and *chin-sheng* or *i-sheng* (the production which is already produced) are equally real. If the former is to be produced or can be produced, then the latter in principle will be produced again and again. So there will be infinite regress. Also, if both *wei-sheng* and *i-sheng* are equally already real, then the one cannot be produced if the other is not produced. Therefore, production cannot be established.

Again, to say that an effect is already real in a cause and that that which is not yet produced will be produced but the product which is already produced will not be produced [again] is unintelligible. For that which is not yet produced and that which is already produced are both real; [they have the same nature]. There is no reason [for them to have different functions], for the one to be produced and the other not.

> COMMENT: The opponent may argue that *wei-sheng* and *i-sheng* are the same only with respect to "essence" or nature but are different with respect to "function"; *wei-sheng* and *i-sheng* cannot (a) both be produced or (b) both not be produced as Nāgārjuna argued in the preceding two paragraphs. To deal with this objection, Nāgārjuna wants to point out that there is no ontological ground for *wei-sheng* and *i-sheng* to have different functions. If two things have the same essence, they should have the same function. So it is untenable to say that *wei-sheng* can produce but *i-sheng* cannot.

Again, if that which is not yet produced is truly real,[1] then that which is already produced would [by your logic] be unreal. Why? Because that which is already produced and that which is

not yet produced are opposite. Since that which is already produced and that which is not yet produced are opposite their
production should be different.

> COMMENT: In previous paragraphs it is argued that if the opponent
> holds that *wei-sheng* and *i-sheng* are equally real, he should not make a
> distinction between them by saying that the one can be produced and
> the other cannot. In this paragraph Nāgārjuna argues that if the opponent,
> on the other hand, holds that *wei-sheng* and *i-sheng* are different and
> that *wei-sheng* is real, it would go against common sense to say that
> *i-sheng* is unreal. For two different things should have two different
> appearances or essences; if one is real, the other should be unreal. This is
> absurd, and therefore it is untenable that an effect is already real in a
> cause and then becomes a product.

Again, real and unreal are opposite.[2] Suppose that which is
produced is real and that which is not yet produced is also real.
Then the two should not be different. Why? If both are real, what
is the difference between them? But it is not true that they are
not different. So if [an effect is] real [in a cause], there can be
no production.

Again, whatever is real has already been realized, why must
it be produced again? Just as that which has been done need
not be done again, and that which has been achieved need
not be achieved again, so what is real would not be produced
again.

Again, if an effect is real in a cause, then the effect should be
observable before it is produced, but actually it is not observable.
For example, the jar should be seen in the clay and the straw mat
in the straw, but in fact they are not observable. Therefore, if
[an effect is] real [in a cause], there is no production.

Question: [But] although an effect pre-exists, it has not yet
undergone change and hence is not observable.

Answer: If when the jar has not been produced, its form has not
undergone change and hence it cannot be observed, by what mark
do we know and say that the jar pre-exists in the clay? Is it by a
jar mark, a cow mark or a horse mark we claim there is a jar? If
the clay does not contain a jar mark, nor a cow mark nor a horse

mark, is it not the same as saying that the jar does not exist? Therefore, it is not tenable to say that an effect pre-exists in a cause and will be produced.

Again, a thing which has undergone change is called an effect, and hence change must have already occurred in the cause. Why? Because you claim that an effect pre-exists in a cause. If things such as jars have undergone change and pre-existed [in their causes], they should have been observable. But in fact they were not observable. Therefore it is unjustifiable to say that an effect has not undergone change and hence is not observable.

If what has not undergone change is not called an effect, an effect is ultimately unobtainable. Why? Because change does not occur before [production] nor does it occur after [production]. So effects such as a jar are ultimately unobtainable.

If what has been changed is called an effect, then an effect is not in a cause. Thus you are uncertain about whether an effect is already in a cause or is not in a cause.

Question: Change pre-exists but cannot be seen. A thing may actually exist although its existence is unobservable. For example, a thing is not perceived because it is too close; or it is not perceived because it is too far away; or it is not perceived because of sensory defect; or it is not perceived because we fail to notice it. A thing cannot be known because of obstacles or because of similarity. It cannot be seen because it is overwhelmed by something else. And a thing may be too small to be known. Medicine in the eye is an example of a thing which is not seen because it is too near. A bird flying high and disappearing in the sky is an example of a thing which cannot be seen because it is too far. Some examples in which a thing cannot be known because of sensory defects are: the blind cannot see colors; the deaf cannot hear; the stopped nose cannot smell; the mouth of a sick person cannot taste; the paralyzed body cannot feel; the crazy mind cannot know reality. An example of a thing which is not known because we do not pay attention to it is this: when we concentrate on certain colors or other things we do not hear a voice. Instances in which a thing is not known because of obstacles are these: the earth blocks [the view of] floods and a wall blocks [the view of] objects. An example of a thing not known because of similarity is a black spot on a black color. An example of a thing not known because it is overwhelmed by another is that we do not hear a soft voice when bells and drums play. An instance of a thing not known because of its small size is that we do not see dust. Thus although things exist, they may not be known because of these eight causal conditions. It is not right for you to say that, just as a jar cannot be found in its cause, so cause cannot contain change. Why? An object may exist and yet is not observable because of the eight causal conditions.

Answer: The fact that changes and effects such as a jar cannot be observed, has nothing to do with the eight causal conditions. Why? Changes and effects which are too near to be seen, would be observable if they were not too near; and those which are too far away to be observed, would be observable if they were nearer. Although our mental faculties are not good enough to observe them, they would be observable if our faculties were pure and good. Although the mind is too inattentive to observe them, they could be observed if the mind were attentive. Obstacles may keep us from seeing something, but changes and effects can be seen when there are no obstacles. When objects are similar, they may not be perceived, but when dissimilar, they can be perceived. When objects are overshadowed they may not be perceived, but when not overshadowed they can be perceived. An object may be too small to be seen, but jars and other effects are big and can be seen.

If a jar is too small to be perceived [in its cause], it could not be perceived after it is produced. Why? Because what is already produced and what is not yet produced have the same characteristic of smallness, for they are both real.

COMMENT: If an effect such as a jar is too small to be seen, it would not be seen even after it has been produced. For *wei-sheng* and *i-sheng* have the same essence. As they have the same essence, they should have the same appearance. So if one cannot be seen, the other will not be seen.

Question: An object is small when it is not yet produced, but it becomes large after it has been produced. Therefore, that which is already produced is observable, while that which is not yet produced is not observable.

Answer: If this is the case, a cause does not include an effect because there is nothing large in the cause.

Again, there is nothing large in the cause before [production]. If there is something large in the cause, you should not say that the effect is too small to be seen. Now the effect is large, yet you say it is too small to be seen; then what is large cannot be called an effect. So an effect ultimately cannot be obtained. Yet actually the effect can be obtained. [Then you should admit that] it is not too small to be seen. [Thus your position is really inconsistent or contradictory.] Therefore, it is not justifiable to say that a cause includes an effect and that, because of the eight causal conditions, the effect cannot be observed.

Again, if a cause includes an effect and then produces the effect, both the cause and the effect lose their characteristics. Why? It is just like a blanket in threads or a piece of fruit in a utensil. The so-called cause would be only a location and cannot be called a cause. Why? Because the thread and the utensil are not the causes of the blanket and the fruit. If a cause is destroyed, the effect will be destroyed. So [in this sense] a thing such as a thread is not the cause of a thing such as a blanket. If there is no cause, there will be no effect. Why? Because of a cause, an effect can be established. If a cause cannot be established, how can an effect be established?

Again, if there is no making, nothing can be called an effect. Causes such as threads cannot produce effects such as blankets. Why? It is that the threads do not produce the blanket just because they provide a place for the blanket. Thus there is neither cause nor effect. If there is neither cause nor effect, one should not seek whether cause includes effect or does not include it.

Again, assume that a cause includes an effect and [grant that the substance of] the effect is not observable. But the characteristics of the effect should be observable. For example, we smell a fragrance and know there are flowers; we hear sounds and know there is a bird; we hear the sound of laughter and know there is a man; we see smoke and know that there is fire; we see the crane and know that there is a pond nearby. Thus, if a cause includes an effect, there should be some signs. Now neither the substance nor the characteristics of an effect are obtainable. So we should know that a cause does not have an effect included in it.

Again, if a cause has an effect included in it and then produces the effect, one should not say that threads cause a blanket nor that straws cause a mat. If a cause does not produce an effect, nothing can produce it. For example, if a blanket is not made by threads, can it be made by straws? If it is not made by threads or straws, shouldn't we say that it is not produced? If it is not produced, we cannot call it an effect. If there is no effect, then there is no cause, as has been pointed out before. Therefore, it is not true that a cause has an effect included in it and then produces the effect.

Again, if an effect is not made [by anything], then it is permanent like *nirvāṇa*. If the effect is permanent, all created things are permanent. Why? Because all created things are effects. If all things are permanent, then there is no impermanence. If there is no impermanence, there is no permanence. Why? Because of permanence there is impermanence, and because of impermanence there is permanence. Thus there is neither permanence nor impermanence. But this is impossible. Therefore one should not say that a cause has an effect included in it and produces the effect.

Again, if a cause has an effect included in it and produces the effect, then the effect would cause another effect. For example, a blanket would cause sitting, a cloak would cause hiding and a cart would cause loading. But in fact these effects are not so caused. Thus one should not say that a cause has an effect included in it and produces the effect.

Someone may argue that earth has a certain good smell, but without rain the smell does not come out. An effect is just like this: [given it is already included in a cause] it would not occur without a combination of conditions. But [I contend that]

this is untenable. Why? As you [the opponent] say, since something is called an effect only after it has been made, then things
such as a jar would not be effects. Why? Because what has been
made has been made. But [by your logic] things such as jar are
already real and cannot be those which are made. Thus, if an
effect is what has been made, it is not justifiable that a cause has
an effect included in it and produces the effect.

Again, the illuminating cause [3] can illuminate but cannot
produce objects. For example, when a lamp is lighted to illuminate
a jar in the dark, it also illuminates the bed and other things [but
cannot produce them]. The conditions which are gathered to
make a jar cannot produce a bed and other things. Therefore one
should know that a cause does not have an effect included in it.

Again, if an effect is already real in a cause and then is produced,
one should not make a distinction between what has been made
and what is yet to be made. But you do make this distinction.
Therefore, it is not true that a cause already includes an effect and
produces it.

> COMMENT: Nāgārjuna has argued that his opponent confuses the
> illuminating cause with the producing cause. Both his examples of rain
> and a lamp would be illuminating cause, not producing cause.
>
> Nāgārjuna has now finished examining the assumption that an effect
> is already real in a cause or that a cause includes an effect and produces
> it. In the following paragraphs, he discusses the assumption that an effect
> is at the outset unreal in a cause or that a cause does not include an effect
> and produce it. He presents several arguments to refute the assumption.

Now assume that a cause does not have an effect included in
it and produces the effect. This is not tenable either. Why? If
something is produced from nothing, then a second head and a
third hand should be produced. Why? Because something could be
produced from nothing.

Question: Things such as a jar have causal conditions [and
hence can be produced]. But a second head and a third hand do
not have causal conditions, so how can they be produced? Therefore, what you say is not right.

Answer: A second head, a third hand, a jar and other effects are all not real in their causes. For example, there is no jar in clay and there is no jar in stone. Why do we call clay, not stone, the cause of a jar? Why do we call milk the cause of cheese, and call yarn, not grass, the cause of a rug?

Again, if a cause does not have an effect included in it and yet produces the effect, then anything can produce anything else. A finger should also produce carts, horses, food and other things. Similarly, yarn should produce not only rugs, but also carts, horses, and food. Why? If something can be produced from nothing, why does yarn produce only rugs, but not carts, horses, food and other unrelated things, since none of them is real in the cause?

If the cause does not include the effect and yet produces it, then the cause should not have a certain distinct and particular power to produce a certain [distinct and particular] effect. [Usually] if we want oil, we get it from sesame, not from sand. But if they have no relation to one another, why do we get oil from sesame and not from sand?

Perhaps you would say that we have been sesame produce oil, but have never seen sand produce it. Therefore, we seek oil from sesame, not from sand. But this is not tenable. Why? If the mark of production is established, then one can say that since we have seen sesame produce oil but have never seen sand produce oil, we seek oil from sesame but not from sand. However, the mark of production has not been established, and hence one cannot legitimately claim that since we have seen sesame produce oil, we seek oil from sesame, not from sand.

Again, what I am doing now is not only refuting one instance of causation, but all causes and effects. That a cause has an effect included in it and produces it, that a cause does not have an effect included in it and produces it, and that a cause both has and does not have an effect included in it and produces it, cannot be established. Your example, that you have seen sesame produce oil, is based on the very idea of causation which is yet to be established.

COMMENT: Nāgārjuna points out that the observation of the constant

conjunction of certain events in the past does not guarantee that similar
events will produce similar effects unless we *assume* the principle of
causality, the very principle which we want to prove. He examines not
a particular causal law in a particular instance, but the very idea of
causation, to show that the universal principle of causality cannot be
justified on empirical grounds.

Again, if a cause does not have an effect included in it and yet
produces the effect, the characteristic of cause cannot be established. Why? If a cause has nothing [included in it], how can it
make anything? How can it produce or achieve? If there is no
making and no producing, how can it be called a cause? Thus
[really], a maker cannot make anything and what is made cannot
make anything either.

If a cause has an effect included in it, then there should be no
distinction between making, a maker and that which is made. For
if the effect is already real, why should it be made again? So you
may say that since making, a maker, that which is made and other
causes cannot be established, [I have to accept the thesis that]
a cause does not have an effect included in it. However, this is
not necessarily true. Why? If one accepts the distinction between
making and a maker and [the reality of] causality, he has to
accept your charge. But I say that making, a maker and causality
are all empty. Furthermore, your refutation of making, a maker
and causality verifies my position, and should not be called against
me. Thus I still maintain that the thesis, that a cause does not
include an effect and then produces the effect, is untenable.
Again, if someone accepts that a cause includes an effect, your
charge is a charge against him. But I do not say that a cause has
an effect included in it, hence I do not have to accept your charge,
and also I do not have to accept the thesis that a cause does not
have an effect included in it.

COMMENT: Nāgārjuna stresses that he does not hold any view and that
the denial of affirmation does not entail the assertion of negation. When
he denies that a cause includes an effect, he does not necessarily assert
that a cause does not include an effect.

He also points out that the opponent's hypothetical charge verifies his position. For the opponent at this point of the argument will grant that it is untenable that cause includes an effect and then produces it. That has been Nāgārjuna's intent in the first half of the chapter.

Nāgārjuna has finished the examination of the second possible view of causal relation. In the following paragraphs, he discusses the third possible view, namely, that a cause both includes and excludes an effect and then produces the effect. He also wants to refute this view.

It is also untenable that a cause can both include and exclude an effect and then produce the effect. Why? Because including and excluding are contradictory in nature. How can things which are contradictory in nature be together? Just as brightness and darkness, suffering and pleasure, going and staying, binding and loosening cannot be together, so a cause which both includes and excludes an effect cannot produce. Again, a cause which [both] includes and excludes an effect has been refuted previously when we examined including and excluding cases [individually].

Therefore, if a cause has an effect included in it, there is no production. If a cause does not have an effect included in it, there is no production either. This is also true of a cause that both includes and excludes an effect. Reasoning can go no further; we have examined all aspects and cannot find [production]. Therefore, the effect is ultimately not produced.

Since the effect is ultimately not produced, all created things are empty. Why? Because all created things are causes and effects.

Since created things are empty, non-created things are also empty.

Since even created and non-created things are empty, is it not more so with the self?

III. CONDITIONS

According to the Abhidharma School, all *dharmas* are real, and are produced by four conditions: (1) the cause-condition (*yin-yüan, hetu-pratyaya*), which acts as the primary cause, for example, the wind and water that cause the wave; (2) the sequential condition (*tz'u-ti-yüan, anantara-pratyaya*) which makes one event occur after another, such as waves that follow each other; (3) the appropriating condition (*yüan-yüan, ālambana-pratyaya*) which is the objective or subjective environment, as concurring cause; for example, waves are conditioned by the basin or the boat or the pond; and (4) the upheaving condition (*tseng-shang-yüan, adhipati-pratyaya*) which brings all conditions to the climax, such as the last wave that upsets the boat. Nāgārjuna examines the four conditions in this chapter.

Again, the conditions of things cannot be established. Why?

> Briefly and broadly,
> conditions do not contain effect.
> If there is no effect within conditions,
> how can it be claimed to come from conditions? [1]

Effects such as a jar are not in any of the conditions nor are they in their aggregate. If they are not in either, how can they be said to come from the conditions?

Question: What are those conditions?

Answer:　Four conditions produce things;
　　　　　there is no fifth condition.
　　　　　[They are] the cause-condition,
　　　　　the sequential condition.
　　　　　the appropriating condition
　　　　　and the upheaving condition [2].

The so-called four conditions are the cause-condition, the sequential condition, the appropriating condition and the upheaving condition. The cause-condition is called so because it produces effects, such as what is already produced, what is being produced and what will be produced. The sequential condition is called so because it makes one event occur after another. The appropriating condition is called so because it provides the subjective setting, like body-*karma*, mouth-*karma* and qualities of the mind. The upheaving condition is that by which other things are culminated. With respect to the others, this is the upheaving condition.

These four conditions show that a cause[3] does not include an effect. If there were an effect in a cause, the effect would exist even without conditions[4]. But in fact there is no effect without the conditions. If an effect were in the conditions, there would be effect without cause. But, in fact, there is no effect without cause. It might be assumed that there is an effect within [both] conditions and causes. But after rational analysis, this is shown unprovable. Therefore, both instances come to naught. Thus, effect is neither in each individual condition nor in their combination. How can it be asserted that effect comes from conditions?

Again,

> If effect does not exist within conditions
> and yet comes from the conditions,
> can it not come from non-conditions?[5]

If it is said that effect is not within conditions and yet is produced by the conditions, why is it not [also] produced by non-conditions? Because it does not exist in either; therefore, there are no such things as causal conditions which can produce effect.

Since effect is not produced, conditions are not produced. Why? Because conditions are prior to effect. Since conditions and effect do not exist, all created things are empty. Since created things are empty, non-created things are also empty. Since created and non-created things are both empty, can there be a self?

IV. CHARACTERISTICS

相 (*hsiang*) in Chinese *sūtras* can be the translation of the Sanskrit terms *lakṣaṇa, nimitta* or *ābhāsa. Lakṣaṇa* means characteristic, mark, sign, aspect or appearance. It usually means the individual characteristic or mark by which one object is distinquished from another. *Nimitta* means appearance or tangible form; and *ābhāsa* is image or shadow. *Hsiang* in this context means primarily the characteristic, mark, sign, property, appearance or visible form of things.

In this chapter Nāgārjuna wants to show that all things are devoid of characteristics, marks, or properties. The same issue is discussed in Chapter VII of the *Middle Treatise*.

Again, all things are empty. Why?

> Neither created nor non-created things
> have characteristics.
> Since they have no characteristics,
> they are both empty.

Created things are not formed by characteristics.

Question: What are created characteristics?

Answer: Everything has certain created characteristics. For example, the horn of an ox is sharp and the tip of its tail has hair; these are characteristics of an ox. The bottom of a jar is flat, its bowl is big, its neck is small, its mouth is round, its edge is rough; these are characteristics of a jar. Wheel, axle, shaft and yoke are the characteristics of a wagon. A man has a head, eyes, body, spine, shoulders, elbows, hands and feet as his characteristics. [Now I ask] if origination, duration and destruction are the characteristics of created things, are they created or non-created?

Question: What is wrong with saying that characteristics are created things?

Answer: If origination is a created thing,
       it should have three characteristics.
       If origination is a non-created thing,
       how can it be called a created characteristic? [1]

If origination is a created thing, it should have the three characteristics [of origination, duration and destruction], and these three characteristics should have three other characteristics, to infinity. This applies also to duration and destruction. If origination is a non-created thing, how can that which is non-created be the characteristic of a created thing? Who can know origination without origination, duration and destruction? Again, origination, duration and destruction are differentiated and hence there is origination. But non-created things cannot be differentiated into origination, duration and destruction, and hence cannot have origination. This also applies to duration and destruction.

Origination, duration and destruction are empty. Therefore created things are empty. Since created things are empty, non-created things are empty, for there are non-created things because of created ones. Now since created and non-created things are empty, all things are empty.

> *COMMENT*: In the argument that follows, Nāgārjuna focuses on origination. The characteristics of duration and destruction can be examined and refuted in the same way.

Question: You say that the three characteristics [each] have three other characteristics, and hence there is an infinite regress. So origination cannot be a created thing. [But] one should say:

> The origination of origination
> comes from the primal origination.
> [On the other hand], the primal origination
> is originated by the origination of origination. [2]

When a thing originates there are seven phenomena: (1) thing, (2) origination, (3) duration, (4) destruction, (5) origination of origination, (6) duration of duration and (7) destruction of destruction. Among these seven phenomena, primal origination

can originate six other phenomena besides itself. And the origination of origination can originate primal origination. Then primal
origination originates the origination of origination again. Therefore, although these three characteristics are created, they do not
involve an infinite regress.[3] This is also the case with duration and
destruction.

    Answer: If it is said that the origination of origination
                originates the primal origination,
                how can the origination of origination
                originate primal origination
                if itself is originated by primal origination?[4]

If it is said that the origination of origination can originate the
primal origination, how can the origination of origination originate
the primal origination when the primal origination has not originated the origination of origination?

    If it is said that the primal origination
    originates the origination of origination,
    how can the primal origination
    originate the origination of origination
    if itself is originated by the origination of origination?[5]

To say that primal origination can originate the origination
of origination, and that the origination of origination which is
already originated can originate primal origination, cannot be true.
Why? The origination of origination should originate primal
origination, and hence is called the origination of origination. But
the primal origination has not yet been originated, so how can it
originate the origination of origination?

To say that while the origination of origination is being originated, it can originate primal origination, cannot be true either.
Why?

    When the origination of origination is being originated
    it may originate primal origination.
    How can it originate primal origination
    if itself has not yet been originated?[6]

When the origination of origination is being originated, it may originate primal origination. But the origination of origination itself has not yet been originated and hence cannot originate the primal origination.

To say that when the origination of origination is being originated it can originate itself and also originate others, just as when light is lighting it can illuminate itself and others,[7] cannot be true. Why?

> There is no darkness in the light
> nor is there darkness in that place.
> The elimination of darkness is called illumination.
> Now what could the light illuminate?[8]

The body of light itself has no darkness. The illuminated place has no darkness either. If there is no darkness in the light nor darkness in the location, how can one say that light illuminates itself and other things? The elimination of darkness is called illumination. [But] the light does not eliminate its own darkness nor the darkness of other things. Therefore it illuminates neither itself nor other things. Thus your statement that, just as light illuminates itself and other things, so origination originates itself and other things, is untenable.

Question: When the light is being lighted, it can eliminate darkness. Therefore, there is no darkness in the light or in the location.

Answer: How can darkness be eliminated
> by the light being lighted,
> when the light, just being lighted,
> does not come in contact with darkness?[9]

If the light cannot come in contact with darkness when it is being lighted, and if it does not come in contact with darkness, one should not say that it eliminates darkness.

Again,

> If the light can eliminate darkness
> while having no contact with darkness,

then the light here
should eliminate all darkness.[10]

If it is said that, although the light does not come in contact with darkness, its power can eliminate darkness, the light here should eliminate all the darkness of the world, for all the darkness does not come in contact with the light. But actually if you light a lamp here, it cannot eliminate all the darkness of the world. Therefore, your thesis that although the light does not come in contact with darkness, it can destroy darkness, is untenable.
Again,

If the light illuminates itself and other things
then darkness will also cover itself and other things.[11]

If you say that light illuminates both itself and other things, darkness, which is contrary to light, should cover both itself and other things. If darkness, which is contrary to light, cannot cover itself and other things, it is incorrect to say that light can illuminate both itself and other things. Therefore, your example is incorrect. One should say,

If origination is not yet originated,
how can it originate itself?
If it is already originated and then originates itself,
why should it need originating?[12]

When this origination is about to originate, it is either like that which is already originated or like that which is not yet originated, and then originates. If it is like that which is not yet originated and then originates, how can it originate itself, since what is not yet originated is not yet in existence? If it is said that it is like that which is already originated and then originates itself, why should it need originating? In it there is no more originating activity, and in that which is made there is no more making activity. Therefore, origination does not originate itself. If origination does not originate even itself, how can it originate other things? It is wrong for you to say that origination originates itself and other things. The case is the same with duration and destruction.

Therefore, the thesis that origination, duration and destruction are created characteristics is not right. Since the thesis that origination, duration and destruction are created characteristics cannot be established, created things are empty.

Created things are empty, therefore non-created things are empty. Why? The destruction of created things is called non-created *nirvāṇa*. Therefore *nirvāṇa* is empty.

Again, no origination, no duration and no destruction are claimed to be characteristics of non-created things. But nothing exists without origination, duration and destruction. That which is non-existent cannot be characteristic of anything.

It may be said that "no characteristic" is the characteristic of *nirvāṇa*, but this is untenable. If "no characteristic" is the characteristic of *nirvāṇa*, by what characteristic do we know it as "no characteristic"? If we know "no characteristic" by a certain characteristic, why is it called "no characteristic"? If we know "no characteristic" by no characteristic, it is not knowable since no characteristic does not exist.

It may be said that it is like clothes which have character, but one garment has no character; it has "no characteristic" as its characteristic. If someone says to bring the one with no characteristic, we know this can be done.[13] Similarly, origination, duration and destruction are characteristics of created things. Whenever there are no-origination, no-duration and no-destruction, we can know they are characteristics of non-created things. Therefore, a state of lacking characteristics is *nirvāṇa*. But this thesis is untenable. Why? Various causal conditions like origination, duration and destruction are empty. Created characteristics cannot be established. How can one claim that non-created things are knowable? By what [other] determinate characteristics of created things do you know that lack of [those] characteristics shows the existence of a non-created thing? Your thesis, that the one with no characteristic among all the clothes is an example of the "no characteristic" of *nirvāṇa*, is untenable. [The issue involved in] the example of clothes will be discussed in detail in Chapter V.

Therefore created things are all empty. Since created things are empty, non-created things are empty. Since created and non-created things are empty, the self is empty. These three are empty and hence all things are empty.

V. WITH OR WITHOUT CHARACTERISTICS [1]

In this chapter Nāgārjuna argues that the characterization or description of anything is empty. He classifies all things into the characterizable (可相 k'o-hsiang) and characteristics (相 hsiang). Metaphysically, the distinction between the two is a distinction between substance and attribute. Grammatically, it is a distinction between a subject and a predicate. Linguistically, it is a distinction between the part of a sentence which serves to identify or designate an object being discussed and that part which serves to describe or characterize the object. Nāgārjuna points out that one who indulges in conceptualization and has the dualistic way of thinking, e.g., divides things into those with characteristics and those without characteristics or into the characterizable and characteristics, will not have an accurate perception and understanding of reality.

Again, all things are empty. Why?

> There is no functioning of characterization
> in the case of a thing with characteristics.
> Nor is there functioning of characterization
> in the case of a thing without characteristics.
> Besides these, what can characteristics characterize? [2]

There is no function of characterization where things have characteristics. Why? If things already have characteristics, why do they need more characteristics? Again, if there were functioning of characterization in the case of things with characteristics, there would be a mistake of having two [kinds of] characteristics: the characteristics which are already possessed by things and the characteristics which are to be used to characterize things. Therefore, there cannot be functioning of characterization when things have characteristics. [3]

Nor can there be functioning of characterization when things have no characteristics. What can be lacking characteristics and yet be characterized by characteristics? An elephant has two tusks, a long trunk, a large head, ears like plates, spine like an arrow, a large belly, hair at the tip of its tail, four strong round feet; these are characteristics of an elephant. Without these characteristics there would be no elephant to be characterized. A horse has raised ears, a mane, four hooves and fine hair in its tail. Without these characteristics there would be no horse to be characterized. Thus there is no functioning of characterization either when things have characteristics or when they do not. Other than the existence and the non-existence of characteristics, there is no third possibility where characterization can occur. Therefore there is no functioning characterization.[4]

Since there is no functioning characterization, there cannot be the characterizable. Why? Because of characteristics something can be called the characterizable. [But] owing to causal conditions, characteristics and the characterizable are empty.[5] Since characteristics and the characterizable are empty, all things are empty. Why? [Because] there cannot be anything without characteristics and the characterizable. Since entities[6] do not exist, there cannot be nonentities.[7] The destruction of an entity is called the non-existence of something. [But now] if the entity does not exist, what is to be destroyed? What is to be called nonentity? Both entity and nonentity are empty. Hence all created things are empty. Since created things are empty, non-created things are empty. Since created and non-created things are empty, the self is also empty.

VI. IDENTITY OR DIFFERENCE

In this chapter Nāgārjuna continues to examine critically the functioning of characterization or description of things. He argues that a conceptual description of reality is impossible by showing that the adequate relation between the characterizable and characteristics cannot be established.

Nāgārjuna's analysis is concerned with what Western philosophers would call substance-attribute relations. He questions the view that a thing or object consists of a substance and attributes. He points out that the so-called substance and attributes are empty for they are neither identical nor different from each other.

Linguistically, the problem of characterization is the problem of predication. In this and previous chapters Nāgārjuna is questioning the adequacy of our language or verbal statements. In both metaphysical and ordinary uses of language a statement usually consists of a subject and a predicate. Nāgārjuna wants to show that the relationship between the subject and the predicate cannot be adequately established. Hence, predication is really impossible.

Again, all things are empty. Why?

> Characteristics and the characterizable
> are neither the same nor different.
> If they are neither the same nor different,
> how can both be established?

Characteristics and the characterizable are neither identical nor different from each other. If their sameness and difference cannot be established, neither can be established. Therefore characteristics and the characterizable are empty. Since characteristics and the characterizable are empty, all things are empty.

Question: Characteristics and the characterizable have always been established. Why can they not be established? You say that characteristics and the characterizable are neither the same nor different. Now you should say that the characteristics of anything

81

are either identical to, or different from, the characterizable; or things may be partially characteristics and partially the characterizable. For example, the characteristic of consciousness[1] is being conscious; without the act of being conscious there is no consciousness. The characteristic of sensation[2] is sensing; without the act of sensing there is no sensation. So characteristics are identical to the characterizable.

The Buddha says that the cessation of desire is called the characteristic of *nirvāṇa*. Desire is created *āsrava*[3]; cessation is non-created *anāsrava*.[4] A believer has three characteristics: he wants to be with good men, he is eager to hear truth and he wants to give alms. These three are the *karmas* of body and mouth, and belong to outward appearances.[5] But belief is of the mind and belongs to mental activities.[6] Here characteristics and the characterizable are different from each other.

Right view[7] is a characteristic of the [Eightfold Noble] Path, and is partially the same as the [Eightfold Noble] Path. Origination, duration and destruction are the characteristics of created things; they are partially the same as created things. Thus the characterizable is partially identical with characteristics.

COMMENT: The Eightfold Noble Path is composed of eight factors: namely, (1) right view, (2) right thought, (3) right speech, (4) right action, (5) right livelihood, (6) right effort, (7) right mindfulness and (8) right concentration. The eight factors are not to be followed and practiced one after the other in numerical order, but to be exercised and developed simultaneously. They are all linked together and each helps the cultivation of the others. So the opponent claims that right view is a characteristic of the Eightfold Noble Path and is also partially the same as the Eightfold Noble Path, and argues that the characterizable is partially identical to characteristics.

So characteristics are either the same as, or different from, or partially the same as the characterizable. Your thesis that since sameness and difference cannot be established, characteristics and the characterizable cannot be established, is untenable.

Answer: Your thesis that characteristics are the characterizable, just as with consciousness and so forth, is not tenable. Why?

Because that which can be known through characteristics is called the characterizable; what has been used in knowing is called characteristics. [But] a thing cannot know itself. For example, a finger cannot touch itself and an eye cannot see itself. Therefore your thesis that consciousness is both a characteristic and the characterizable is untenable.

Again, if characteristics are the same as the characterizable, there is no distinction between them. If we make a distinction, we should not say that they are the same.

Again, if characteristics are the same as the characterizable, cause and effect would be one. Why? Characteristics are cause and the characterizable, effect; two are one. But in fact they are not one. Therefore, it is not right to say that characteristics and the characterizable are the same.

Your thesis is that characteristics and the characterizable are different from each other is also untenable. You say that the cessation of desire is the characteristic of *nirvāṇa*, not that desire is the characteristic of *nirvāṇa*. If it is said that desire is the characteristic of *nirvāṇa*, then the characteristic is different from the characterizable. If it is said that the elimination of desire is the characteristic of *nirvāṇa*, then it should not be said that the characteristic is different from the characterizable.

You also say that a believer has three characteristics. [But in fact] a believer and the three characteristics are not different from each other. [For they are related in such a way that] if there is no belief there are no three events. Therefore, characteristics and the characterizable cannot be different. Moreover, if characteristics and the characterizable are different, a characteristic can have other characteristics, and there would be an infinite regress; but this is impossible. Therefore, characteristics and the characterizable cannot be different.

Question: Just as the light can illuminate itself and other things, so characteristics can characterize themselves and other things.

Answer: Your example of the light has been refuted previously when we discussed three created characteristics. Besides you seem to contradict your own former view: previously you said that characteristics and the characterizable were different, but now you say that characteristics can characterize themselves and other things. This is untenable.

Again, you say that the characteristics are part of the characterizable. This is untenable. Why? Because the meaning lies in sameness or in difference. But the meanings of sameness and difference have been refuted previously. So you should know that the view that the characteristics are part of the characterizable should be refuted.

Thus, characteristics and the characterizable of various causal conditions are neither identical nor different from each other. There is no other possibility. Therefore, characteristics and the characterizable are both empty. Since both are empty, all things are empty.

VII. BEING OR NON-BEING

This chapter discusses four characteristics; namely, origination, duration, change and destruction. Being (*yu*) in this context refers to origiantion and duration, and non-being (*wu*) refers to change and destruction. Nāgārjuna argues that these four characteristics cannot be established. He also wants to assert that the teachings given by the Buddha cannot be grasped by an interplay of concepts, such as being and non-being or existence and non-existence.

Again, all things are empty. Why? Being and non-being are neither obtainable at the same time nor at different times.[1] As it is written,

There cannot be being with non-being;
nor can there be being without non-being.
If there can be being with non-being,
then being should always be non-being.[2]

Being and non-being are contradictory to each other in nature. One thing cannot include both of them. For example, when there is life there is no death. When there is death there is no life. This has been discussed in the *Middle Treatise*. You may say that there is no mistake [in the view that] being exists without non-being. But this is not the case. Why? How can there be being without non-being! As pointed out previously, when something is produced the seven phenomena are produced together.[3] As stated in the *Abhidharma*, being and impermanence are produced together. Impermanence is the characteristic of destruction and hence is called impermanence. Therefore, without non-being [and its characteristic, impermanence], being cannot be produced. If being can be produced with impermanence, then being would always be

non-being. If being is always non-being, duration cannot be originated, because permanence is destroyed. But in fact there is
duration. Therefore being is not always non-being. [And to say]
that being can be produced without impermanence cannot be
true either. Why? Without impermanence being really cannot be
produced.

Question: When being is produced, impermanence is already
included in it and yet does not go into action. When there is
destruction, impermanence goes into action and being is destroyed.
Thus, origination, duration, destruction and decay have to wait for
their time to go into action. At the beginning [of production],
origination is effective and hence being is originated. Between
origination and destruction, duration is effective and hence being
is upheld. At the end, impermanence is effective and hence being
is destroyed. Decay is a change from origination to duration and
from duration to destruction. Impermanence destroys permanence
and this makes the four phenomena possible. Therefore, although
a thing is produced with impermanence, being is not always
non-being.

Answer: You say that impermanence is also the characteristic of
destruction and is produced with being. Then at the time of being
produced, being is being destroyed; and at the time of being
destroyed, being is being produced.[4]

Again, there cannot be production and destruction. Why? At
the time of being destroyed, there cannot be production. And at
the time of being produced, there cannot be destruction, for
production and destruction are contradictory.

Again, you say that impermanence and duration are produced
together. [But] at the time of destruction, there cannot be duration, and at the time of duration there cannot be destruction.
Why? Because duration and destruction are contradictory.

At the time of decay[5] there is no duration, and at the time
of duration there is no decay.

Therefore, your thesis that impermanence is originally with
origination, duration, destruction and decay is absurd. Why? Suppose that being is produced with impermanence. Impermanence is

the characteristic of destruction. When a thing is produced it has no characteristic of destruction and when it exists it has no characteristic of destruction either. When, then, can there be impermanence?

Because of "being conscious", there can be consciousness; without being conscious there can be no characteristic of consciouness. Because of "being able to sense" there can be sensation; without being able to sense, there can be no characteristic of sensation. Memory can be called such because of "being able to remember"; there can be no characteristic of memory without being able to remember. Origination is a characteristic of production; non-origination is not a characteristic of production. Endurance is a characteristic of duration; non-endurance is not a characteristic of duration. Change is a characteristic of decay; no change is not a characteristic of decay. Destruction of life is a characteristic of death; no destruction of life is not a characteristic of death. Thus, destruction is a characteristic of impermanence. Without destruction there is no characteristic of impermanence.

COMMENT: Nāgārjuna refutes the opponent's argument by pointing out that whatever can be conceived to exist must, in principle, be cognizable, observable or verifiable. Nothing can be said to exist if there is no distinguishing mark or sign by which we know of its existence. So the idea of the existence of impermanence is unintelligible if it does not have any distinguishing mark or characteristic (destruction) which is capable of being perceived. One should not say that origination and impermanence are produced together at the same time since at the time of origination nothing is capable of being observed as "impermanence".

Suppose that although there is impermanence, it does not destroy being at the time of origination and duration, but it will later. Why are they produced together? It is only at the time when being is destroyed that impermanence is needed. So it is incorrect to say that impermanence is produced together with being and later destroys it.

Thus the unity of being and non-being cannot be established, nor can their disunity. Therefore, being and non-being are empty.

Since being and non-being are empty, all created things are empty. Since all created things are empty, non-created things are empty. Since created and non-created things are empty, all sentient beings are also empty.

VIII. NATURE

Nature (性 *hsing*) here refers to essence, self-nature or fundamental nature behind a manifestation or expression. Nāgārjuna wants to show that the characteristic of nature cannot be established, and hence to demonstrate that all things are empty. Nāgārjuna also argues that the doctrine of emptiness is not nihilism and does not make Buddhism impossible. Instead, the doctrine is given to save, or account for, empirical phenomena and religious practices.

Again, all things are empty. Why? Because things have no nature. As it is written,

> By observing that the characteristics [of all things] change
> We know all things are devoid of nature.
> Things which are devoid of nature are also non-existent,
> so all things are empty.[1]

If things have a nature, they should not be changing. But we see that all things are changing. Therefore we know that they are devoid of nature.

Again, if things have a determinate nature, they should not be produced by conditions. If nature is produced by conditions, then it is that which is made.[2] [Yet] nature [as defined] is that which is not made and not causally dependent upon other things.[3] Therefore, all things are empty.

Question: If all things are empty, then there can be no origination or destruction. If there are no origination and destruction, then there can be no truth of suffering. If there is no truth of suffering, there can be no truth of the arising of suffering. If there are no truths of suffering and its arising, there can be no truth of the cessation of suffering. If there is no cessation of suffering, there can be no way leading to the cessation of suffering. If all things are empty and without nature, there can be no four noble

89

truths. If there are no four noble truths, there can be no four
fruits of *śramaṇa*.[4] If there are no four fruits of the *śramaṇa*,
there can be no sainthood. If there are none of these things, there
can be no Buddha, *Dharma* and *Saṅgha*,[5] and there can be no
principle of worldly affairs. But these are not so. Therefore, things
cannot all be empty.[6]

Answer: There are two truths; namely, conventional truth and
ultimate truth. Because of conventional truth, ultimate truth is
attainable. Without relying on conventional truth, ultimate truth
cannot be attained. Without attaining ultimate truth *nirvāṇa*
cannot be attained.[7] If one does not know two truths, he cannot
know self-interest, other-interest and common interest.[8] Thus, if
one knows conventional truth, he then knows ultimate truth, and
if one knows ultimate truth, he knows conventional truth.[9] Now
you hear of conventional truth and call it ultimate truth, and
hence become lost. The doctrine of causation given by buddhas
is called the profound truth. Causation is devoid of self-nature,
and hence I say [all things are] empty.

If things are not produced by conditions, they should have
their own determinate nature.

There can be no marks of origination and destruction in the five
skandhas. If there is no origination and no destruction in the five
skandhas, there can be no impermanence.[10] If there is no impermanence, there can be no noble truth of suffering. If there is no
noble truth of suffering, there can be no noble truth of the arising
of suffering. If things have a determinate nature, there can be no
noble truth of the removal of suffering. Why? Because natures
cannot be changed. If there is no noble truth of the removal of
suffering, there can be no way leading to the removal of suffering.
Therefore, if we do not accept the doctrine of emptiness, there
can be no four noble truths. If there are no four noble truths,
there can be no possession of the four noble truths. If there is
no possession of the four noble truths, there can be no such
things as knowing suffering, eliminating the cause of suffering,
proving the removal of suffering and cultivating the way leading
to the removal of suffering. If those things cannot be, there can

be no four fruits of *śramaṇa*. If there are no four fruits of *śramaṇa*, there can be no goal [for the religious life]. If there is no goal, there can be no Buddha. If the truth of causation is denied, there can be no *Dharma*. If there is no *Dharma*, there can be no *Saṅgha*. If there are no Buddha, *Dharma* and *Saṅgha*, then there can be no Three Jewels. If there are no Three Jewels, the principle of the world is denied. But this is absurd. Therefore all things are empty.[11]

Again, if things have determinate natures, there can be no origination, no destruction, and no good or evil. If there is no reward or punishment for good and evil, the world can be but one scene. Therefore, we should know that things have no nature.[12]

If it is argued that things have no self-nature and are made from other-nature, this cannot be true either. Why? Because if there is no self-nature, how can they come into being from other-nature, for owing to self-nature there is other-nature.[13]

And other-nature is [a kind of] self-nature too. Why? Because other-nature is the self-nature of others.[14]

If self-nature cannot be established, other-nature cannot be established either. Without self-nature and other-nature, how can there be anything? If being cannot be established, non-being cannot be established either.[15]

Now we infer, therefore, that since there is no self-nature, no other-nature, no being and no non-being, all created things are empty.

Since created things are empty, non-created things are empty. Since even created and non-created things are empty, what of the self?

IX. CAUSE AND EFFECT

In the first few chapters of the treatise Nāgārjuna examined the concept of causation and argued that cause and effect are devoid of any nature. In this chapter he stresses that the marks of causal phenomena cannot be established, for the marks of effect cannot be in any causal condition nor in their combination. Nāgārjuna also argues that since the mark of effect cannot be established, effect is empty. And if effect is empty, all things are empty because all things are products (effects) of other things.

Again, all things are empty. Why? Things by themselves have no nature; nor do they come from elsewhere. As it is written,

Within all conditions effect is ultimately unobtainable.
Nor does it come from elsewhere.
How can there be an effect?[1]

As stated previously, there is no effect within any one of the conditions nor within the unity of all conditions. Effect does not come from elsewhere either. If it comes from elsewhere, it would not be produced by causal conditions. And the combination of various conditions would have no function.[2] If effect is not in conditions and does not come from elsewhere, it is empty.

Effect is empty, so all created things are empty. Created things are empty and hence non-created things are empty.

Even created and non-created things are empty: consider then the self as also empty.

X. THE CREATOR

The opening verse denies the four possible ways of viewing the cause of suffering; that is, self-caused, other-caused, both self-caused and other-caused, and non-caused. The term other (他 | *t'a*) here and in the rest of the chapter means anything other than itself or oneself. It may refer to a person or persons as well as a thing or things. In what follows, Nāgārjuna uses the logic of *reductio ad absurdum* to show the absurdity and untenability of each causal view. In doing this, he repudiates the concept of God as the creator and savior.

Again, all things are empty. Why? Because it is impossible for a thing to be made by itself, by another, by both [itself and another], or from no cause at all. As it has been said,

It is not justifiable
that suffering is made by itself,
by another, by both or from no cause at all.
Therefore there is no suffering.[1]

Suffering cannot make itself. Why? If it makes itself, it makes its own substance. But a thing cannot use itself to make itself. For example, consciousness cannot be conscious of itself, and a finger cannot touch itself. Therefore nothing can be said to make itself.

Suffering is not made by another either. How can it be made by the other?

Question: Conditions are called other. Conditions make suffering: this is called "to be made by other". How can you say suffering is not made by other?

Answer: If conditions are called other, suffering is made by conditions. If suffering is produced from conditions, then it has conditions as its substance. If it has conditions as its substance, why are the conditions called other? For example, in a clay jar, clay is not called other; in a golden bracelet, gold is not called other. This also applies to the case of suffering. If it is produced by conditions, the conditions cannot be called other.

Again, conditions do not have self-nature. They are not self-existent. Therefore it cannot be said that effect is produced from conditions. As it has been written in the *Middle Treatise*,

> Effect is produced from conditions,
> [but] conditions are not self-existent,
> If conditions are not self-existent,
> how can conditions produce effect?

> COMMENT: This is taken from verse 13 of Chapter I of the *Middle Treatise*. According to Piṅgala, whatever can be conceived to exist must have a certain nature or self-nature. If causal conditions do not have self-nature, they cannot be conceived to exist. And if the conditions are non-existent, how can we say that effect is produced by them?

Thus suffering cannot be made by other. Nor can it be made by both itself and other, for this involves two fallacies. If you say that suffering is made by itself and by other, then there would be the fallacies of self-made *and* other-made [which have both been refuted]. Therefore it is not justifiable that suffering is made by both.

That suffering is produced from no cause at all cannot be true either, for that involves that fallacy of eternalism.[2]

As it is written in the scripture, a naked Tīrthika asked the Buddha, "Is suffering made by itself?" The Buddha kept silent and did not answer. "World-honored![3] If suffering is not made by itself, is it made by other?" The Buddha still did not answer. "World-honored! Is it then made by itself and by other?" The Buddha still did not reply. "World-honored! Is it then made by no cause at all?" The Buddha still did not answer. Thus, as the Buddha did not answer these four questions, we should know that suffering is empty.

> COMMENT: A Tīrthika is a heretical or non-Buddhist religious man.

There were six famous Tīrthikas: namely, Pūraṇa-Kāśyapa, Maskarin, Sañjayin, Ajita-kesakāṁbala, Kakuda-Kātyāyana, and Nirgrantha. The naked Tīrthikas, according to the Chinese master T'ai-hsü, belonged to the Nirgrantha sect of naked devotees who abandoned all ties and forms.

Question: Buddha's teaching in the scripture is not that suffering is empty, but he did this for the sake of saving sentient beings.

COMMENT: This exchange juxtaposes Hīnayāna and Mahāyāna views. According to Hīnayānists, the Buddha kept silent when non-Buddhists such as the Tīrthika asked him about the cause of suffering because they had prejudices and false views in mind before they asked the questions. Unless they abandoned their prejudices, they could not understand the truth, so the Buddha did not answer. In fact, suffering is real, not empty. But according to the Mādhyamika, the real reason the Buddha kept silent was that all things are empty and cannot be expressed or discussed in the form of the four alternative views.

Answer: The Tīrthikas say that man is the cause of suffering. Those who believe in the real existence of the self say good and evil are made by the self.[4] The self is clean and pure and has no suffering and troubles. That which knows and understands is the self. It makes good, evil, suffering and happiness, and is embodied in various forms. Since they have those wrong views and ask the Buddha, "Is suffering made by itself?" the Buddha does not answer. Suffering is really not made by the self.

If the self is the cause of suffering, suffering is produced owing to the self. The self would be impermanent. Why? If things are causes and produced from causes they are all impermanent.[5] Now if the self is impermanent, then the fruits and the consequences of good and evil [deeds] would disappear. The performance of Brāhmanic deeds to obtain good rewards would also be empty.

COMMENT: The self or *ātman* is supposed to be permanent. Nāgārjuna points out that if the self is the cause of suffering it would be impermanent, and therefore the opponent's view involves a contradiction. *Empty* in the last sentence suggests "would eventually disappear". Traditional religious practice would be in vain.

If the self is the cause of suffering, there can be no liberation.

Why? If the self makes suffering, without suffering there will be no self which is the maker of suffering; if there is no self, then who will achieve liberation? If suffering can be made without the self, there will be suffering even after liberation; and there is no [real] liberation. But in fact, there is liberation. Therefore, it is not justifiable that suffering is made by itself.

Suffering is not made by other either. If suffering is separated [from the other], how can there be another self who makes suffering and bestows it on the recipient?

> COMMENT: This involves two absurdities: (a) without suffering itself there is nothing that can be called "other". (b) without suffering, who is going to be the recipient to receive suffering? Reasoning here is similar to the argument in the *Middle Treatise* XII: 5 and 6.

Again, "Suffering is made by other" may mean it is made by God (Iśvara). Some who hold this heterodox view asked the Buddha [about the creation of the universe]. So the Buddha did not answer. Really it was not made by God. Why? Because [God and suffering (the universe)[6]] are contradictory in nature. A calf born of a cow is still a cow. If creatures are created by God, they should be similar to God. For they are His sons.

> COMMENT: 自在天 (*Tzu-tsai-tien*) literally means "self-existing Heaven)". It refers to Iśvara, the title of Siva, the king of the *devas* or gods. Here Nāgārjuna uses the self-existing Heaven of Iśvara to examine the concept of God and to show that God cannot be used to explain the origin, duration and destruction of the universe.

Again, if God created all living beings, He would not give them suffering. Therefore one should not say that God created suffering.

Question: All living beings are created by God, and suffering and happiness are also given by God. But they do not know the cause of happiness, and hence God gives them suffering.

Answer: If all living beings are the sons of God, He should use happiness to cover suffering and should not give them suffering.

And those who worship Him should not have suffering but should enjoy happiness. But this is not true in reality. They act by themselves and have happiness and suffering, and receive rewards according to the principle of causal conditions. All these are not made by God.

COMMENT: Nāgārjuna has presented the problem of evil to question whether God is all good. In the next paragraphs, he questions whether God is self-sufficient, self-caused and omnipotent, and touches on predestination.

Again, if God is self-existent, He should need nothing. If He needs something, He should not be called self-existent. If He does not need anything, why did He [cause] change, like a small boy who plays a game, to make all creatures?

Again, if God created all living beings, who created Him? That God created Himself, cannot be true, for nothing can create itself. If He were created by another creator, He would not be self-existent.

Again, if God is the [omnipotent] creator, there should be no obstacle to the process of His creation; He could make [everything] in just one instant. [But] the scripture about God says: God wanted to create all creatures. He practiced various ascetic deeds and then created all creeping insects. Again He practiced ascetic deeds and then created all flying birds. Again He practiced ascetic deeds and created men and *devas*. [7] If it were a result of the practice of ascetic deeds that creeping insects were first produced, and then flying birds, then men and *devas*, we should know that living beings were produced from *karmas* of causal conditions, not from God who practiced ascetic deeds. [8]

Again, if God is the creator of all creatures, where did He create them? Was the place [where He performed creation] created by Him? Was it created by another? If it was created by God, then where did He create it? If He stayed in another place to create this place, then who created the other place? Thus there would be an infinite regress. If that were created by another, there would then be two Gods, but this cannot be true. Therefore all things in the universe are not made by God.

Again, if God is the creator, why should He practice ascetic deeds as if He were worshipping and pleasing another in order to attend to His wish? If He has to practice ascetic life to beg the other's favor, we should know God is not self-existent.

Again, if God created all things, things should be determinate [in nature] at the beginning of creation and should not be changing.[9] A horse is always a horse and a man is always a man. But now all things are changing according to *karma*. Therefore we should know that all things are not made by God.

Again, if God is the maker [of all things], there should be no sinfulness and blessedness because good, evil, beauty, and ugliness are all made by God. But actually there is sinfulness and blessedness. Therefore all things are not made by God.

Again, if all living beings come from God, they should respect and love Him just as sons love their father. But actually this is not the case; some hate God and some love Him. Therefore we should know that all things are not made by God.

Again, if God is the maker [of all things], why did He not create men all happy or all unhappy? Why did He make some happy and others unhappy? We would know that He acts out of hate and love, and hence is not self-existent. Since He is not self-existent, all things are not made by Him.

> COMMENT: What Nāgārjuna wants to say seems to be this: God can neither be all good nor self-sufficient. If he is all good, why did He not create all men happy? If He is self-sufficient, why did He make some happy and others unhappy? Also, why does He worry about whether He should love or hate them? Since God cannot be all good or self-sufficient, the traditional God, the divine being, cannot exist.
>
> In the next three paragraphs, Nāgārjuna questions the belief that man's fate and salvation are made and controlled by God. He argues that the belief is empirically unjustifiable and also makes moral and religious practices impossible.

Again, if God is the maker [of all things], all living beings cannot have made [anything]. But, actually each living being has skillfully made something. Therefore, we should know that all things are not made by God.

Again, if God were the maker, good, evil, suffering and happiness would come without being made [by men]. But this would destroy the principle of the world [that men do good and obtain reward, and do evil and receive punishment]. The practice of an ascetic life and Brāhmanic deeds would be in vain. But this is not the case. Therefore, we know that all things are not made by God.

Again, if God is great among sentient beings according to causal conditions, then all sentient beings who practice the *karma* of happiness [10] should also be great. Why is God only honored? If God is self-existent without causal conditions, then all sentient beings should [in principle] be self-existent. But actually this is not the case. So you should know that all things are not made by God. If God [has a cause and] comes from another, then this other may come from still another. There will be an infinite regress. If there is an infinite regress, there can be no cause.

Thus, there are various causal conditions which make things. You should know that all things are not made by God and also that God does not exist. When a person who held this heterodoxical view asked the Buddha about suffering being made by another, he did not answer.

COMMENT: This paragraph summarizes the discussion of the impossibility of something made or produced by other. In the following paragraphs Nāgārjuna examines the last two alternative views of making — made by both self and other, and made by neither — and argues that they cannot be established.

It cannot be the case that something is made by both [itself and other] either, for this [as has been shown] has two fallacies.

The combination of causal conditions produces all things, so nothing is produced from no cause. The Buddha did not answer this [question] either.

[Question]: Therefore the scripture only refutes four wrong views and does not say that suffering is empty.

COMMENT: This statement, supposedly made by the opponent, claims that the silence of the Buddha is only the denial of the four possible ways of viewing things. It does not imply that all things are empty.

In the closing paragraphs, Nāgārjuna insists that the silence of the Buddha is the same as the teaching of the doctrine of emptiness. He reaffirms the main teaching of the Mādhyamika; namely, that *pratītyasamutpāda* or dependent origination is the same as *śūnyatā*.

Answer: Although the Buddha says a combination of causal conditions produces suffering, to refute the four wrong views is the same as saying suffering is empty. If suffering is produced from causal conditions, it means that suffering is empty. Why? Because anything which is produced by causal conditions has no self-nature. Anything which lacks self-nature is empty.

If suffering is empty, you should know that created, non-created and all sentient beings are empty.

XI. THE THREE TIMES

In this chapter Nāgārjuna examines the three temporal relations, namely, earlier than, later than and simultaneous with. He attempts to show that the production of particular things is impossible because it cannot occur in any temporal moment and because a temporal relation between events cannot be established. This chapter ends his discussion of the possibility that a *particular* object or event can be causally produced. In his last chapter Nāgārjuna will argue that production *as such* cannot be established.

Again, all things are empty. Why? A cause is neither earlier than, later than, nor at the same time as an effect. As it has been said,

"Earlier than", "later than" and "simultaneous with"
such events are impossible.
How can events be produced by causes?[1]

It cannot be true that a cause is prior to an effect. Why? If a cause exists earlier and from it an effect is produced later, there would be no effect initially, and what would be its cause? If an effect is prior to a cause, then the effect has already been established when there is no cause, and why must it need a cause? If a cause and an effect exist at the same time, there would be no causal production either. For example, the horns of a cow are produced simultaneously; the left and the right do not cause each other. Then the so-called cause cannot be the cause of the effect, and the so-called effect would not be the effect of the cause, for they are produced at the same time. Therefore the three temporal relationships between cause and effect are unattainable.

COMMENT: Causal production must be performed in certain temporal relationships: a cause is either earlier than, later than or simultaneous with an effect. But Nāgārjuna wants to show that the temporal moments

101

of priority, posteriority and simultaneity are empty: hence the functioning of causal production cannot be established. Since causality is empty,
all things are empty. For all things are causes and effects. Nāgārjuna's
analysis of the three times and his argument for their emptiness are
intended to demonstrate that all things are empty.

Question:[2] Your refutation of causation cannot be established
in the three temporal relationships either. If refutation is prior to
the refutable,[3] then there would not be the refutable and what
could refutation refute? If the refutable is prior to refutation, then
the refutable has been established, and why does it need to be
refuted? If refutation and the refutable exist at the same time,
there would be no causal [relationship between them]. For
example, the horns of a cow are produced at the same time;
the left and the right do not cause each other. Thus refutation
does not cause the refutable, and vice versa.

Answer: Your refutation and the refutable have the same kind
of mistake.

If all things are empty, there can be neither refutation nor
that which is to be refuted. Now you say that my refutation is
empty; this establishes what I say.

If I say that there must be refutation and the refutable, I
would be mistaken, as you claim; but I do not say there must be
refutation and the refutable, so I should not be troubled by your
charge.

COMMENT: The Mādhyamikas often claim that they do not hold any
position or have any viewpoint of their own. What they are doing is
simply using what other people believe to point out that the opponent's
viewpoint involves certain contradictions or absurdities. Their refutation
and criticism of the opponent's theory are not a negation of something
which is real; nor is it done for the sake of the affirmation of their own
viewpoint, but as a complete negation. It does not presuppose anything;
for them, all "affirmations" and "negations" should be given up. Therefore Nāgārjuna claims that the opponent's refutation and criticism of
his refutation of others' theories, do not trouble him, but rather support
what he says.[4]

Question: We do observe that a cause is prior to an effect; for example, a craftsman makes a jar. A cause could also be later than an effect; for example, because of disciples there is a master, and they are known as the disciples [only] after teaching takes place. A cause and an effect may also exist at the same time; for example, the light and its brightness exist at the same time. So it is not right to say that a cause is neither prior to, nor later than, nor at the same time as an effect.

Answer: Your example of a craftsman making a jar is not a correct one. Why? If there is no jar [yet], what would the craftsman be the cause of? As with the craftsman, nothing can be a cause prior to an effect.

It is also untenable that there is a cause which is later than an effect. If there is no disciple, who can be a master? Therefore, a cause which is later than an effect is untenable.

If you say that like light and brightness, cause and effect exist at the same time, you still maintain a doubtful cause.[5] Suppose the light and its brightness exist at the same time, how can they cause each other?

Thus causes and conditions are empty. Hence you should know that all created things, non-created things and all sentient beings are empty.

XII. PRODUCTION

The term *sheng* literally means production or origination. It can also refer to making, doing, acting, changing and creating. In this chapter, Nāgārjuna examines the concept of *sheng* as such and shows that it is an empty term. The function of production, originating, making, doing, acting, changing and creating cannot be established.

The way Nāgārjuna treats the concept of *sheng* is similar to his analysis of the concept of change or motion in Chapter II of the *Middle Treatise*. He divides the path or passage of production into (a) that which is already produced, (b) that which is not yet produced, and (c) that which is being produced. He exhibits that none of the three moments can be established and thereby demonstrates that production is really empty.

It should be noted that there is no clear-cut distinction between active and passive moods in Chinese. *Sheng* as a verb means "to be produced" and "to produce". So (a), (b) and (c) in this context can be that which has produced, that which has not yet produced or does not produce, and that which is producing, respectively.

Again, all things are empty. Why? Because that which is already produced, that which is not yet produced and that which is being produced are unattainable. What is already produced is not to be produced. What is not yet produced is not produced yet. What is being produced is not to be produced either. As it is said,

> The effect already produced is not to be produced;
> that not yet produced is not produced.
> Without that which is already produced
> and that which is not yet produced,
> that which is being produced is not produced.[1]

That which is already produced refers to the effect which has already arisen. That which is not yet produced refers to what has not yet arisen, does not come out or does not exist. That which is being produced refers to what is just arising but is not yet accomplished.

Among them the product of production is not to be produced. This is [partially] due to the fact that what is already produced is not to be produced. Why? Because it would involve the fallacy of an infinite regress, the reproducing of what is done. If that which is already produced produces a second product, this second product which is already produced would produce a third product, and then the third product which is already produced would produce a fourth. This is just like the original product which has already had the second product and then produces infinite products; but this is impossible. Therefore that which is already produced does not produce.

Again, if you say that which is already produced produces, what it uses to produce is that [part] which is not yet produced. But this is impossible. Why? Because to use what is not yet produced to produce involves two kinds of production; namely, what is already produced is produced and what is not yet produced is produced. Your position seems to be shifting and uncertain.

It is like this: what has been made need not be made; what has been burned need not be burned; what has been proven need not be proved. Thus what has been produced need not be produced. Therefore what is already produced is not to be produced.

The thing which is not yet produced [2] is not produced either. Why? Because it has no connection with production. [3] Also there would be the fallacy that all [effects] which are not produced are produced. If that which is not produced is produced, there would be producing without production. Therefore there is no production.

If there is producing without production, then there would be creating without creation, there would be departing without departure and there would be consuming without consumption. This destroys the principle of the world [that is, it is against common experience] and is untenable. Therefore, the thing which is not yet produced is not produced.

Again, if the thing which does not produce produces, then all things which do not produce should produce. All ordianry people who do not produce enlightenment (*Anuttara-samyak-sambodhi*) would produce enlightenment;[4] an indestructible *arhat* who does not generate evil passion would generate evil passion; and a rabbit and a horse which do not grow horns would grow horns. But these are impossible. Therefore you should not say that that which does not produce produces.

Question: That which does not produce produces [only] when it has a certain combination of causal conditions. If causal conditions such as time, place, a maker and skillful means are all present, some of that which does not produce will produce, but not all will produce. So you should not refute me by saying that all should produce.

Answer: Suppose that which does not produce produces when it has a combination of appropriate conditions such as time, place, a maker and skillful means. There is no production when it pre-possesses [a product].[5] Nor is there production when it does not pre-possess [the product]. Nor is there production when it both pre-possesses and does not pre-possess [the product]. Thus production is unattainable in all three instances as pointed out before.[6] Therefore that which does not produce will not produce.

That which is producing does not produce either. Why? Because it involves the fallacy that what has already produced produces [again], and also the fallacy that what has not yet produced produces. It has been discussed previously that what has produced, a part of what is producing, does not produce. It has just been discussed that what has not yet produced, the [other] part of what is producing, does not produce either.

> COMMENT: That which is producing is supposed to be between (a) that which has produced and (b) that which has not yet produced; in another view, (a) and (b) are considered its parts. Thus, that which is producing depends on that which has produced and that which has not yet produced. If the latter are denied, the former must be denied.

Again, if there is that which is producing without production, then that which is producing produces. But actually without production there cannot be that which is producing. Therefore, that which is producing does not produce.

Again, if anyone says that there is production in that which is producing, then there would be two productions: (1) that which is producing is produced, and (2) that which is producing produces. But neither of these two can be established, so how can one say there are these two productions? Therefore there is no production in that which is producing.

Again, without production there is not that which is producing. Where would the production be performed? If there is no place where that production is produced, then there cannot be that producing. Therefore that which is producing does not produce.[7]

Thus, that which is already produced, that which is not yet produced, and that which is being produced cannot be established. Since production as such cannot be established, origination, duration and destruction cannot be established either.

Since origination, duration and destruction cannot be established. Created things cannot be established. Since created things cannot be established, non-created things cannot be established. Since created and non-created things cannot be established, all sentient beings cannot be established.

Therefore you should know all things have no production; they are ultimately empty and tranquil.

NOTES

One Nāgārjuna scholar has translated *Shih-erh-men-lun* (十二門論) as *Twelve Topic Treatise*. I prefer *Twelve Gate Treatise*, for the word *men* (門) literally means gate; it is a way to get out of some place and to enter into another, and *shih-erh*, twelve, is a perfect number for the Chinese. The title *Twelve Gate Treatise* fits the original purpose of the book, namely, that it is designed as the perfect way to get rid of extreme views and enter into the right view.

According to tradition, the verses of the *Middle Treatise* are given by Nāgārjuna, but their explanations are given by Piṅgala (青目). The verses of the *Hundred Treatise* are given by Āryadeva, but their explanations are given by Vasu (提婆). However, in the *Twelve Gate Treatise*, both verses and explanation are given by Nāgārjuna.

The Preface and Table of Contents are given by Seng-jui, whose dates are 352–436.

TABLE OF CONTENTS [SENG-JUI]

1 This can also be rendered as causal relation, relational condition, conditioning cause or causality.

2 性 (*hsing, svabhāva*) is the fundamental nature or essence behind manifestation or expression.

3 The four conditions are the cause-condition, the sequential condition, the appropriating condition and the upheaving condition; see Chapter III.

4 相 (*hsiang, lakṣaṇa*) means mark, characteristic, sign, indication, designation.

5 The three characteristics are origination, duration and destruction.

6 "An object and characteristics" are 可相 (*k'o-hsiang*), the subject, and 相 (*hsiang*), the predicate.

7 The four characteristics are origination, duration, change and destruction.

8 Four cases are: made by itself, made by other, made by both itself and other, and made by neither itself nor other.

108

9 The three times are earlier than, simultaneous with, and later than.

10 生 (*sheng, utpāda*) means production, origination, beget, birth, begin.

PREFACE [SHENG-JUI]

1 折 (*che*) literally means snap, cut or prune. Here it means to refute erroneous or extreme views, or to prune inessentials. 中 (*chung*) literally means
center, middle, moderation. Here it means to expound or to illuminate something correctly. It also means to bring out essentials. According to Chi-tsang,
che-chung is "to prune things and make them straight or harmonious".
(*Commentary on the Twelve Gate Treatise*, T. 1825, p. 171a.)

2 實相 (*shih-hsiang*) literally means the true mark, the reality, but here it
primarily means emptiness or the middle way. The opening phrase can be
rendered as "The *Twelve Gate Treatise* is to expound correctly the doctrine
of emptiness by refuting extreme views". It might also be rendered, "*The
Twelve Gate Treatise* is the concise summary of the doctrine of emptiness".

3 道場 (*tao-ch'ang, bodhimaṇḍala*) literally means the field or place of
enlightenment. Here it refers to right observation or enlightenment.

4 In his *Early Mādhyamika in India and China*, Richard Robinson translated
yüan and *li* as "the source or the one source" and "the principle or the one
principle", respectively (p. 208).

5 If translated literally, "there would be deviations, attached inclinations".

6 Literally, "no matter (*shih*) is unexhausted". In the previous paragraph,
Seng-jui talks about *li* (理); in this paragraph, he mentions *shih* (事). *Shih*
is phenomenon and activity, in contrast with *li*, which is theory, the underly-
ing principle, noumenon or essence. The ideas of *shih* and *li* later become
important philosophical concepts in the Hau-yen and T'ien-t'ai Schools,
and Neo-Confuncianism.

7 筌 (*ch'uan*). The term *fishtrap* comes from the *Chuang-tzu*, 26.

8 *Reliance* here means the reasons which serve to support the doctrine of
emptiness. It also means the devices which are used to show the emptiness of
all things.

9 The terms 造次 (*chao-tz'u*) are taken from the *Analects* Book IV: Chapter
V.

10 兩玄 (*liang-hsüan*) also means double profundity. Here it refers to the emptiness of emptiness or the doctrine of emptiness. These Chinese terms are taken from the *Tao-te-ching*, Chapter I. Seng-jui used Taoist and Confucian terms and phrases to explain Buddhist teachings.

11 Or eliminate erroneous views in one destination. 一致 (*i-chih*) also come from the *Tao-te-ching*, Chapter XXXIX. They mean one destination or unity. The terms 顛沛 (*tien-p'ei*) come from the *Analects* Book IV: Chapter V.

12 恢恢 (*hui-hui*) literally means great or broad enough to embrace everything. The phrase comes from the *Chuang-tzu*, 3, 2a, 4b.

13 The phrase comes from the *Tao-te-ching*, Chapter XIV.

14 和鸞 (*ho-luan*), according to Chi-tsang, is an imperial carriage which has a phoenix singing in a gentle voice. Here it stands for the Great Vehicle. 'The Northern Ocean' is taken from *Chuang-tzu* 1, 1A. 1a.

15 Chi-tsang comments that "just as when the sun comes out, there is no longer any dark place, so when this treatise is studied, there will be no more doubt and impediment". (*op. cit.*, p. 1746)

16 Literally, "It is not because of any benefit". This can also be rendered, "I have done so not for the benefit of others".

CHAPTER I: CAUSAL CONDITIONS

1 See David J. Kalupahana, *Causality: The Central Philosophy of Buddhism* (University of Hawaii Press, Honolulu, 1975).

2 See Walpola Rahula, *What The Buddha Taught* (Grove Press, New York, 1959). pp. 52—54.

3 義 (*i*) also means meaning, purpose, truth and righteousness.

4 法藏 (*fa-tsang*) is the treasury of Buddha's teaching and the *sūtras*.

5 *Shih-fang*, referring to the eight points of the compass, the nadir and the zenith.

6 *San-shih* or the past, present and future.

7 In the *Middle Treatise* the doctrine of emptiness is spoken of as not for the unintelligent or slow-witted (XXIV: 12).

8 In the *Middle Treatise* Nāgārjuna also pointed out that the unintelligent people have misconceived emptiness and hence ruined themselves (XXIV: 11).

9 Here Nāgārjuna carries on the spirit of the Buddha's compassion as stated at the end of the *Middle Treatise*: "I reverently bow to Gautama, who out of compassion taught this *dharma* in order to eliminate all views". (XXVII: 30)

10 *Tathāgata* is normally interpreted as "thus come", "thus gone", or by some as "he who has come from the truth or absolute". It refers to one who has attained or arrived at the state of truth and is one of the epithets of the Buddha.

11 Literally, "immeasurable and boundless".

12 The two vehicles refer to *śrāvakayāna* and *pratyekabuddhayāna*. The objective of both is personal salvation, while the objective of the Mahāyāna or *bodhisattva* is the salvation of all sentient beings. Thus Mahāyāna is claimed to be superior to the two vehicles.

13 According to Master T'ai-hsü, great men are the men of great virtue and great wisdom. They are the same as buddhas. See T'ai-hsü, *T'ai-hsü-ta-shih-chüan-shu* (*A Collection of Great Master T'ai-hsü's Writings*), Vol. 13 (Great Master T'ai-hsü Committee, Taipei, 1969), p. 617.

14 觀世音 (*Kuan-shih-yin*) means "Regarder of the world's sounds, or cries". Avalokiteśvara was originally represented as a male, but his image was later changed to that of a female figure. Among the Chinese, Avalokiteśvara is known as Kuan-yin, Goddess of Mercy. Kuan-yin is one of the triad of Amitābha, and is also represented as crowned with Amitābha.

15 Mahāsthāmaprāpta is a *bodhisattva* who has obtained great power and stability. He is on Amitābha's right; Avalokiteśvara is on his left. They are called the Buddhist Trinity of Sukhāvati.

16 Mañjuśrī, in past incarnations, is described as the parent of many buddhas and as having assisted Śākyamuni into existence. His title was the supreme Buddha of the Nāgas; now his title is the spiritual Buddha who joyfully cares for the jewel. His future title is to be the Buddha universally revealed. He is usually regarded as the guardian of wisdom and often holds a book, the emblem of wisdom, or a blue lotus. Legends about him are many. In the introductory chapter of the *Lotus Sūtra* he is considered the ninth

predecessor or Buddha-ancestor of Śākyamuni. He appears in military array as defender of the faith. His signs and magic words are found in various *sūtras*. His most famous center in China is Wu-t'ai Mountain in the province of Shansi, where he is the object of pilgrimages.

17 Maitreya is the Buddhist messiah. According to tradition, he was born in Southern India of a Brahman family. He now lives in the Tusita heaven. He will come again some 4000 heavenly years after the *nirvāṇa* of Śākyamuni. He presides over the spread of the Buddhist church, protects its members and will usher in ultimate victory for Buddhism.

18 The six *pāramitās* are charity, moral conduct, patience, devotion, contemplation and knowledge. They are the means of crossing over from this shore of births and deaths to the other shore or *nirvāṇa*.

19 A similar issue is discussed in the *Middle Treatise* 1: 1−2 and 15: 3.

20 有爲法 (*yu-wei-fa, saṁskṛta dharmas*) can also be rendered as conditioned things.

21 我 (*wo, ātman*).

22 比丘 (*pi-chiu, bhikṣu*) means a religious man, an almsman, or one who has left home, been fully ordained, and depends on alms for a living.

23 Self belongings here refer to attributes or properties of the self.

CHAPTER II: WITH OR WITHOUT EFFECT

1 A similar statement is given in the *Middle Treatise* 1: 6. 定有 (*ting-yu*).

2 Literally, "real and unreal (*yu wu*) are contrary to each other; unreal and real (*wu yu*) are contrary to each other".

3 了因 (*liao-yin*).

CHAPTER III: CONDITIONS

1 This verse is similar to the *Middle Treatise* 1: 11. According to Chi-tsang, there are five interpretations of "briefly and broadly": (1) *briefly* refers to the aggregate of all causal conditions and *broadly* refers to each individual condition. (2) Chapter I has been a general examination of causal conditions and hence is implied by *briefly*; Chapter II has been an analysis of the status of effect and hence is called *broadly*. This third chapter examines both conditions and effect, and hence is both. (3) *Briefly* means shortly, and *broadly* means comprehensively. Chapter II discusses causal relation at length and hence has a broad examination of causality. This third chapter does not discuss causal relation at length and hence has a brief examination of causality. (4) *Briefly* refers to the fact that Chapter II studies merely whether an effect is in a cause. *Broadly* refers to the fact that this chapter examines whether an effect is in any of various conditions. (5) *Briefly* means separately and *broadly* means together. This third chapter examines causes and conditions separately and together; it is a brief and broad study of causality. (T. 1825, p. 195a).

2 This verse is almost identical with the *Middle Treatise* 1: 3.

3 Cause here mainly refers to the cause-condition (*hete-pratyaya*).

4 Conditions here refer to the three other conditions.

5 This verse is almost the same as the *Middle Treatise* 1: 12.

CHAPTER IV: CHARACTERISTICS

1 This verse is the same as the *Middle Treatise* 7: 1.

2 The same verse appears in the *Middle Treatise* 7: 4.

3 Piṅgala's commentary on the *Middle Treatise* 7: 4 is identical.

4 This verse is the same as the *Middle Treatise* 7: 5.

5 Same as the *Middle Treatise* 7: 6.

6 Same as the *Middle Treatise* 7: 7.

7 Similar to the *Middle Treatise* 7: 9. In the *Hui-cheng-lun*, 34–41, Nāgārjuna used the example of fire to discuss the similar issue.

8 Same as the *Middle Treatise* 7: 10.

9 This verse is almost the same as the *Middle Treatise* 7: 11.

10 Same as the *Middle Treatise* 7: 12.

11 Same as the *Middle Treatise* 7: 13.

12 Same as the *Middle Treatise* 7: 14.

13 The similar example is discussed by Vātsyāyana under *Nyāyasūtra* 2.2.10; see Bimal Krishna Matilal, *The Navya-nyāya Doctrine of Negation* (Harvard University Press, Cambridge, 1968), Vol. 46, p. 107.

CHAPTER V: WITH OR WITHOUT CHARACTERISTICS

1 有 (*yu*) here also means existence and "to be with". 無 (*wu*) also means non-existence and "not to be with" or "to be without".

2 The last sentence may also be rendered, "there cannot be the functioning of characterization". This verse is quite similar to the *Middle Treatise* 5: 3.

3 According to Chi-tsang, two fallacies are involved: (1) things have already been characterized and need no characteristics, and (2) if they need to be characterized, it will lead to an infinite regress (*op. cit.*, p. 201b).

4 Pingala's commentary on the *Middle Treatise* 5: 3 is similar. (see T. 1564, p. 76b—c).

5 Characteristics and the characterizable are causally co-arising and are devoid of self-nature, hence they are empty. This sentence might also be rendered, "Owing to these reasons, characteristics and the characterizable are empty."

6 物 (*wu*) also means things or objects.

7 無物 (*wu-wu*) also means "there exists nothing" or "nothing exists".

CHAPTER VI: IDENTITY OR DIFFERENCE

1 識 (*shih, vijñāna*).

2 受 (*shou, vedanā*) is one of the five *skandhas*.

3 有漏 (*yu-lou, āsrava*) is whatever has *kleśa*, distress or trouble. It also means mortal life or the stream of births and deaths.

4 無漏 (*wu-lou, anāsrava*) means no drop, leak, flow outside the passion stream, or passionless. It is *nirvāṇa* as contrasted with 有漏 , which is mortality.

5 色陰 (se-yin, rūpa).

6 行陰 (hsing-yin, saṁskāra).

7 正見 (cheng-chien, samyag-dṛṣṭs).

CHAPTER VII: BEING OR NON-BEING

1 This sentence can also be rendered, "Being and non-being are neither together nor separate".

2 This verse comes from verse 19 of the Śūnyatā-saptati.

3 See Chapter IV.

4 "Produced" (生 sheng) can also be rendered as "originated".

5 老 (lao) also means old age.

CHAPTER VIII: NATURE

1 This verse is almost identical with 13: 3 in the Middle Treatise.

2 This sentence is the same as 15: 1b in the Middle Treatise.

3 Similar to the Middle Treatise 15: 2b.

4 The term śramaṇa refers to Buddhist monks or ascetics of all kinds who have left their families and quit the passions. A śramaṇa must keep well the truth, guard well every uprising of desire, be uncontaminated by outward attractions, be merciful to all and impure to none, not elated by joy nor harrowed by distress, and be able to bear whatever may come. The four fruits of the śramaṇa are the four fruitions or rewards resulting from these practices: namely, srota-āpanna-phala, sakradāgāmi-phala, anāgāmi-phala, and arhat-phala, i.e., four grades of sainthood. These four titles are also referred to as the four grades of śramaṇas: namely, yellow and blue flower śramaṇas, lotus śramaṇas, meek śramaṇas and ultra-meek śramaṇas.

5 The Buddha (the enlightened one), the Dharma (his doctrine or teaching) and the Saṅgha (the community of monks or followers) are known as the Three Jewels. For monks and laymen, initiation into Buddhism starts with a proclamation of allegiance, which runs like this:

I take my refuge in the Buddha.
I take my refuge in the Dharma.
I take my refuge in the Saṅgha.

6 The entire paragraph is almost identical with the *Middle Treatise* 24: 1–6.

7 These statements are almost identical with the *Middle Treatise* 24: 8–10.

8 The twofold truth is primarily a teaching device and has three kinds of utility. According to Chi-tsang, self-interest, other-interest and common interest have the following meanings: (1) To comprehend conventional truth and then ultimate truth produces *upāyaprajñā*, the wisdom of using skillful means or expedient knowledge: this is self-interest. To comprehend ultimate truth and then conventional truth produces *prajñāupāya*, the means of attaining wisdom: this is other-interest. To produce these two forms of wisdom is common interest. (2) To have one's own comprehension of the twofold truth and one's own production of the two forms of wisdom is self-interest. To use the twofold truth to help others in understanding the Buddha's *dharma* so as to attain the two forms of wisdom is other-interest. Enlightenment for oneself and others is common interest. (3) To produce *prajñā* by means of the ultimate truth is self-interest. To produce *upāya* by knowing the conventional truth is other-interest. To have both *prajñā* and *upāya* is common interest (*op. cit.*, p. 206b).

9 In the *Middle Treatise* Nāgārjuna points out that ultimate truth needs conventional truth, while here he stresses the mutual dependence. The two truths are dependent on and relative to each other.

10 If the five *skandhas* have determinate nature (定性, *ting-hsing*), they cannot be changed. Hence, there can be no origination, destruction, impermence, etc.

11 The argument here is similar to the reasoning in the *Middle Treatise* 24: 20–30.

12 Nāgārjuna presents a similar argument in the *Middle Treatise* 24: 33–38.

13 The same issue is discussed in the *Middle Treatise* 1: 2b.

14 This is almost the same as the *Middle Treatise* 15: 3.

15 The same reasoning is found in the *Middle Treatise* 15: 4–5a.

CHAPTER IX: CAUSE AND EFFECT

1 This verse appears to summarize Nāgārjuna's argument in the *Middle Treatise* 12:1.

2 The combinations of conditions do have function, so effect cannot come from elsewhere.

CHAPTER X: THE CREATOR

1 This verse is similar to the *Middle Treatise* 12:1.

2 無量 (*wu-liang*) here refers to *śāśvata-vāda* (eternalism).

3 世尊 (*shih-tsun*) is an epithet of every Buddha. This is a translation from "Lokanātha" or "Bhagavat".

4 神 (*shen*) usually means god, divinity or spirit, but here it refers to 神我 (*shen-wo*), which is a self, ego, soul or permanent person.

5 This sentence seems to imply that anything which is a cause or an effect is impermanent.

6 Here Nāgārjuna uses "suffering" as an example of a creature in order to discuss the origin, duration and destruction of the universe.

7 天 (*t'ien*) literally means heaven, but here it is a name for *devas*, gods.

8 Nāgārjuna seems to argue that the idea of God as the omnipotent creator is incompatible with the concept of *karma* and the principle of causal conditions.

9 What is made is supposed not to have the power of self-making, and hence cannot be changed by itself; otherwise it can make itself and should not be said to be made by God or others.

10 福業 (*fu-yeh*).

CHAPTER XI: THE THREE TIMES

1 This verse is similar to the *Middle Treatise* 11:2.

2 The question whether negation must be the negation of something has also been raised in the Hui-cheng-lun, 11–16.

3 可破 (*k'o-p'o*) is the refutable, the object of refutation.

4 The argument is similar to the Hui-cheng-lun, 61—67.

5 疑因 (*i-yin*). The causal relation between them is still doubtful.

CHAPTER XII: PRODUCTION

1 This verse is similar to the *Middle Treatise* 7: 15.

2 未生 (*wei-sheng*) may mean simply "is not produced".

3 This sentence can also be rendered, "It is contrary to production" or "there is no principle of producing in it".

4 *Anuttara-samyak-sambodhi*, also known as *Anubodhi*, is the excellent, complete enlightenment, the highest correct awareness. It is also considered to be the perfect wisdom of a Buddha.

5 Or "when it pre-possesses [causal conditions]".

6 This has been discussed in Chapter II.

7 "Without production" in the first sentence can also be translated as "before production as such is established". According to Chi-tsang's *Commentary on the Twelve Gate Treatise*, that which is producing (*sheng-shr*) must have production as such (*sheng*) as its substance; without *sheng* there can be no *sheng-shr*. So before *sheng* is established, how can one use *sheng-shr* to establish it?

GLOSSARY

Note: S – Sanskrit, P – Pali, Ch – Chinese, Jap – Japanese.

Abhidharma (S), Abhidhamma (P): "Higher doctrine", "super-doctrine" dealing with Buddhist philosophy and psychology; the third division of the Pali canon of scripture.

Amitābha (S), Omito (Ch), Amida (Jap): The Buddha of Infinite Light; the founder of *Sukhāvatī*, the Western Paradise; the object of worship in the Pure Land School.

Anātman (S), Anattā (P): Non-ego, non-self; the denial of the *Ātman* of Hindu philosophy conceived as a personal immortal soul or a substantial self.

Anitya (S), Anicca (P): Impermanence, change.

Anuttara-samyak-sambodhi (S), Anuttara-sammā-sambodhi (P): Unexcelled complete enlightenment; an attribute of every *buddha*.

Arhat (S), Arahant (P): The worthy one; a saintly man, the highest type or ideal in Hīnayāna, comparable to a *bodhisattva* in Mahāyāna.

Asaṁskṛta (S), Asaṃskhata (P): Non-created or unconditioned things.

Ātman (S), Attā (P): Ego, self, soul, or individual personality. In Brāhmanism the Absolute, the unconditioned, the spirit, *Brahman*; also the reflection of the Absolute in the individual.

Avalokiteśvara: The *bodhisattva* representing compassion; in China known as Kuan-yin; in Japan, Kannon.

Avidyā (S), Avijjā (P): Ignorance; lack of enlightenment.

Āyatana (S & P): Sense-fields. There are twelve, corresponding to the six sense faculties (five senses and the mind), and their objects.

119

Bhāvaviveka (Bhavya or Bhāviveka): The founder of the Svātantrika school of the Mādhyamika. He criticized Prāsangika Mādhyamika for merely indulging in refutation without advancing a counter-position and claimed that the true Mādhyamika could consistently advance an opposite view.

Bhūmi (S): Earth; a stage. There are ten successive enlightenment stages of a *bodhisattva*.

Bodhi (S & P): Enlightenment, enlightened mind, perfect wisdom, illumination, intuition, or inner light.

Bodhidharma: The first patriarch of Ch'an Buddhism in China.

Bodhisattva (S), Bodhisatta (P): Wisdom-being. It was first used in the sense of a previous incarnation of the Buddha. Many lives before his final birth as Siddhartha Gautama, the Bodhisattva did mighty deeds of compassion and self-sacrifice, as he gradually perfected himself in wisdom and virtue. In Mahāyāna, the *bodhisattva* is the ideal of the Path comparable to the *arhat* of the Theravāda. He is any individual self-dedicated to the salvation of others and destined to the attainment of buddhahood.

Brahman (S): The Absolute, the ultimate substratum of all things.

Buddha (S & P): The awakened or enlightened one. Siddhartha Gautama after attaining enlightenment. Other individuals who have similarly attained **enlightenment**.

Buddhi (S & P): Enlightenment, intelligence, intuition, the faculty of direct awareness of reality.

Candrakīrti: An important philosopher of Prāsangika Mādhyamika Buddhism of the seventh century. It was due to his efforts that *prasanga* (*reductio ad absurdum*) became the real and only method of Mādhyamika reasoning.

Ch'an (Ch): The Chinese word for *dhyāna*, or meditation. The Ch'an School was founded by Bodhidharma, and is known as Zen Buddhism to the West.

Chi-tsang (Ch): The greatest Chinese San-lun philosopher of the seventh century. He worked in the Chia-hsiang Monastery and was known as Chia-hsiang Ta-shih (the Great Master Chia-hsiang).

Ching (Ch): Scripture.

Ching-t'u Tsung (Ch): The Pure Land School. *Ching-t'u* is a translation of the Sanskrit term *Sukhāvatī* (Land of Bliss). It is called Jodo in Japanese. According to this school, anyone who believes in Amita Buddha will be born in the Pure Land to become a buddha.

Chung-lun (Ch): The *Middle Treatise* (T 1564 in Vol. 30). One of three main texts of the San-lun School. It was translated by Kumārajīva in 409 A.D. from the now lost *Mādhyamika-śāstra*. The main verses were written by Nāgārjuna, and its commentary was given by Piṅgala.

Conditions: There are four: (1) The cause or chief condition (*hetu-pratyaya*) which acts as the chief cause, for example, the wind and water that cause the wave; (2) the sequential condition (*samanantara-pratyaya*) which immediately follows a preceding condition, such as waves following each other; (3) the appropriating condition (*ālambana-pratyaya*) which is the objective or subjective environment as concurring cause, for example, waves are conditioned by the basin or the boat or the pond; and (4) the upheaving condition (*adhipati-pratyaya*) which brings all conditions to the climax, such as the last wave that upsets the boat.

Deva (S & P): A god, angel, or benevolent being.

Dharma (S), Dhamma (P): Truth, law, norm, doctrine, teaching, sermon, righteousness, morality, religion or doctrine; a thing, fact, element, factor, mark, attribute or quality.

Dhātus (S): Element, factor, or constituent.

Dhyāna (S): Meditation, or direct absorption in truth.

Divākara: The master of the Sautrāntika Svātantrika of Mādhyamika Buddhism in the seventh century. He introduced the Sautrāntika Svātantrika to China from India.

Duhkha (S), Dukkha (P): Suffering, sorrow, pain.

Dvādasa-dvāra-śāstra (S): The *Twelve Gate Treatise*. One of the three main texts of San-lun Buddhism.

Eightfold Noble Path: Right view, right thought, right speech, right action, right livelihood, right effort, right mindfulness and right concentration.

Fa (Ch): The Chinese term for *dharma* (S) or *dhamma* (P). A thing, fact, element, mark, truth, law, doctrine, norm, teaching, sermon, morality.

Fa-hsiang Tsung (Ch): Chinese Yogācāra School.

Five skandhas (S): Five aggregates, the sole constituents of personality. They are form (*rūpa*), sensation (*vedanā*), perception (*sañjñā*), impulses (*samskāra*) and consciousness (*vijñāna*).

Four Noble Truths: The four basic principles of Buddhism preached by Buddha in his first sermon:
    1. Duhkha (S), Dukkha (P). Suffering or sorrow.
    2. Samudaya (S & P). The cause of suffering.
    3. Nirodha (S & P). The cessation of suffering.
    4. Mārga (S), Magga (P).The way leading to the cessation of suffering.

Gautama (S), Gotama (P): The clan name of the Buddha's family.

Hīnayāna (P): The Small Vehicle (of achieving *nirvāṇa*), a derogatory appellation given by the Mahāyānists to denote early schools, of which the Theravāda is the sole survivor.

Hsiang (Ch): Mark, characteristic, sign, aspect, appearance, quality or attribute.

Hsing (Ch): Own-nature or fundamental nature behind a manifestation or expression.

Hsüan-tsang (Ch): An important Chinese Buddhist translator and commentator of the seventh century.

Hua-yen Tsung (Ch): Chinese Avataṁsaka School.

Hundred Treatise: The *Pai-lun* (Ch), T 1569 in Vol. 30. It was translated by Kumārajīva in 404 A.D. from the *Sata-śāstra*. Its main verses were given by Āryadeva and its commentary was given by Vasu.

Īsvara (S & P): Overlord, a supreme personal god.

Jih-chao (Sh): The Chinese name of Divākara. He brought Sautrāntika-Svātantrika-Mādhyamika Buddhism to China from India in the seventh century.

Jiriki (Jap): Salvation by one's own efforts.

Jodo (Jap): The Japanese term for *Sukhāvatī*, Pure Land or Land of Bliss.

Karma (S), Kamma (P): Action, work, deed or product; the mysterious power which causes all action to work itself out in requital in another life; moral action which causes future retribution, and either good or evil transmigration.

Karunā (S & P): Compassion; with *prajñā* one of the two pillars of the Mahāyāna.

Kegon (Jap): Japanese Hua-yen School. It was brought to Japan by Dosen in the eighth century.

K'ung (Ch): Emptiness or voidness.

Kumārajīva: A great Buddhist scholar of the fifth century in Central Asia. He introduced Mādhyamika Buddhism to China, and is noted for the number of his translations and commentaries.

Lakṣaṇa (S): Marks, characteristics, properties, or predicates.

Li (Ch): Principle; reason.

Lun (Ch): Treatise.

Lung-shu (Ch): Nāgārjuna.

Lung-shu-p'u-sa-chuan: The *Biography of Bodhisattva Nāgārjuna*, T 2047.

Mādhyamika (S): The Middle-Way School founded by Nāgārjuna, known as San-lun Buddhism in China.

Mādhyamika-kārika. The *Middle-Way Stanzas*, the original text of the Mādhymika teaching written by Nāgārjuna.

Mahāprajñāpāramitā (S): The perfection of great wisdom; the title of a Mahāyāna scripture.

Mahāyāna (S & P): The Great Vehicle (of salvation); the Northern Buddhist School. This school has been popular in China, Korea, Japan, Tibet and Mongolia.

Maitreya: An advanced Bodhisattva who is destined to be the Buddha-to-come. He is often considered to be the Buddhist Messiah. According to tradition, he was born in Southern India of a Brahman family. He now lives in the Tusita heaven. He will come again 5000 or 4000 heavenly years (about 4,670,000,000 human years) after the *nirvāṇa* of Śākyamuni. He presides over the spread of the Buddhist church, protects its members and will usher in an ultimate victory for Buddhism.

Mañjuśri: The Bodhisattva who is considered to be the embodiment of all the Buddhas' wisdom.

Mārga (S), Magga (P): Path or way. It is generally used to describe the Eightfold Noble Path or the Middle Way.

Ming (Ch): Name, symbol.

Mokṣa (S): Liberation from *saṁsāra* and all its pains.

Nāga (S & P): Dragon; elephant; serpent.

Nāgārjuna: The great Buddhist philosopher of the second century. He distinctively taught the Mahāyāna doctrine of emptiness and founded Mādhyamika Buddhism. According to tradition, he discovered many Mahāyāna texts and established the Mahāyāna School of Buddhism, and hence was often called the "father of Mahāyāna".

Nidānas (P): The twelve links in the chain of causation.

Nirodha (S & P): Cessation, extinction, extermination. It often refers to the third noble truth, the cessation of suffering.

Nirvāṇa (S), Nibbāna (P): "Blown out", "gone out", "put out", "extinguished"; liberation from existence; deliverance from all suffering; the supreme goal of Buddhist endeavor. *Nirvāṇa* is a state attainable by right aspiration of life and the elimination of egoism. In the Buddhist scriptures the Buddha speaks of *nirvāṇa* as "unborn, unoriginated, uncreated, unformed", contrasting it with the born, originated, created and formed phenomenal world. The Hīnayāna tends to view *nirvāṇa* as escape from life by overcoming its attraction. The Mahāyāna views it as the fruition of life, the unfolding of the infinite possibilities of the innate buddhanature, and exalts the saint who remains in touch with life, rather than the saint who relinquishes all connection with it.

Pai-lun (Ch): See the *Hundred Treatise*.

Pali (P): One of the early languages of Buddhism. It was later adopted by the Theravādins as the language in which to preserve the memorized teachings of the Buddha.

Pali Canon: The Three Baskets of the Scripture, i.e. *Suttapitaka, Vinayapitaka* and *Abhidammapitaka*, in the Pali language. The Canon contains the main sacred texts of Theravāda Buddhism. It was complied and edited by three monastic councils. The first council assembled just a few months after the death of the Buddha (483 B.C.) in Rajagaha, the second about a hundred years later (around 383 B.C.) in Vesāli, and the third in 225 B.C. in Pātaliputta.

Paramārthasatya (S): Ultimate or absolute truth.

Pāramitā (S & P): Transcendental perfectiom, especially the perfected virtue of a bodhisattva. In Mahāyāna Buddhism, there are usually six major *pāramitās*: charity, discipline, vigor, patience, meditation and intuitive wisdom.

Pitaka (P): Basket. The Buddhist Pali Canon is called the Pitakas or the *Tipitaka* (three baskets).

Prajñā (S), Paññā (P): Wisdom, reason, insight.

Prajñāpāramitā (S): The perfection of wisdom; the designation of a body of Mahāyāna literature.

Pramāṇa (S): The means, source, evidence or proof of true cognition. Four *pramāṇas* are perception, inference, analogy and testimony.

Prāsangika: One of two major Mādhyamika schools. It was founded by Buddhapālita (c. 400–450 A.D.). According to this school, the real and true method of Nāgārjuna and Āryadeva is *prasanga (reductio ad absurdum)*. The true Mādhyamika does not and should not uphold any position of his own.

Pratītyasamutpāda (S), Paticcasamuppāda (P): Dependent origination or arising; causality.

Pratyekabudda (S): "Private" or "lonely" *buddha*, so called because he reaps the fruits of his striving without returning to share that merit with mankind.

Śākyamuni (S & P): The sage or holy man of the Sākyas; a title given to the Buddha by those outside the Sākya clan.

Samādhi (S & P): Meditation, contemplation, concentration, rapture, tranquility.

Saṁsāra (S & P): "Faring on", "coming-to-be"; the world of becoming; the realm of birth and death. *Saṁsāra* is symbolically referred to as "this shore", *nirvāṇa* as "the other shore", and *dharma* as "the raft" which carries us across.

Saṁskṛta (S), Saṁskhata (P): Created or conditioned things and states.

Samudaya (S & P): Cause of suffering; the second noble truth.

Saṁvṛtisatya (S): Conventional, relative or worldly truth.

San-lun Tsung (Ch): Lit. "Three Treatise School". Chinese Mādhyamika Buddhism.

San-lun hsüan-i (Ch): The title of the book, the *Profound Meaning of Three Threatises* (T 1852 in Vol. 45), written by Chi-tsang.

Saṅgha (S & P): The Order, the assembly or congregation of monks and nuns; the third of the three jewels of Buddhism.

San-shih (Ch): Three times — earlier than, simultaneous with and later than.

Sanskrit: The classical Aryan language of India. Most Mahāyāna texts were written in Sanskrit.

Sanron (Jap): Japanese San-lun Buddhism.

Śāstra (S), Satthā (P): Commentaries or independent essays on Buddhist teachings.

Śata-śāstra (S): See the *Hundred Treatise.*

Sautrāntika: Buddhists who hold the *Sūtras* as their authority and not the *Śāstras*. They do not admit the authority of the *Abhidharma* of the Sarvāstivādins. They assert the reality of both physical objects and the mind, but claim that we do not have a direct perception of external objects.

Seng-chao: An eminent Chinese San-lun philosopher of the fifth century. He is the author of the *Chao-lun.*

Seng-jui: An important Chinese San-lun Buddhist of the fifth century. He wrote prefaces to the *Middle Treatise* and the *Twelve Gate Treatise*.

Sheng (Ch): Production, origination, arising.

Shih-erh-men-lun (Ch): The *Twelve Gate Treatise* (T 1568 in Vol. 30); one of the three main texts of San-lun Buddhism. It was translated by Kumārajīva in 408–409 A.D. from the now lost *Dvādasa-dvāra-śāstra*. Both main verses and commentary were given by Nāgārjuna.

Shih-fang (Ch): Ten directions, referring to the eight points of the compass, the nadir and the zenith.

Siddhārtha Gautama (S): Siddhattha Gotama (P): The name of the Buddha, the founder of Buddhism. It was given by his father, King Suddhodana of Kapilavastu.

Six famous Tīrthikas: A Tīrthika is a heretical or non-Buddhist religious man. The six famous Tīrthikas were Pūraṇa-Kāśyapa, Maskarin, Sañjayin, Ajita-kesakambala, Kakuda-Kātyāyana and Nirgrantha.

Six forms of life: Hellish things, hungry spirits, beasts, evil spirits, human beings, and heavenly beings.

Six pāramitās (S & P): Six perfections. They are charity, moral conduct, patience, devotion, contemplation and knowledge.

Six sense organs: Eye, ear, nose, tongue, body and mind.

Skandhas (S), Khandhas (P): Aggregates or heaps. The five *skandhas* are the sole constituents of personality. They are form (*rūpa*), sensation (*vedanā*), perception (*sānjñā*), impulses (*saṁskāra*) and consciousness (*vijñāna*).

Śramaṇa (S): An ascetic, a religious recluse.

Śrāvaka (S): A hearer, disciple of the Buddha who understands the Four Noble Truths, rids himself of the unreality of the phenomenal and enters the incomplete *nirvāṇa*. It is used by Mahāyānists, in conjunction with *pratyekabuddha*, to describe Hīnayānists.

Sukhāvatī (S): Pure land; the goal of the followers of the Pure Land School.

Śūnya (S): Empty, void, vacant, non-existent.

Śūnyatā (S): Emptiness, voidness, non-existence.

Sūtra (S), Sutta (P): Literally, a thread or string on which jewels are strung; a sermon or discourse of the Buddha. It often refers to that part of the Pali Canon containing narratives about dialogues by the Buddha. A number of Mahāyāna scriptures are also called *sūtras*.

Svabhāva (S): Own-nature, self-nature, self-existence, self-being, selfhood, that which does not depend on others for its existence.

Svātantrika: One of the two major schools of Mādhyamika Buddhism. It was founded by Bhāvavivedka in the sixth century. According to this school, empirical things are not real from the standpoint of ultimate truth, yet have phenomenal reality.

Ta-chih-tu-lun (Ch): The *Great Wisdom Treatise* (T 1852 in Vol. 45).

Tariki (Jap): Salvation by some "other power".

Tathāgata (S & P): "Thus-gone" or "Thus-come", "He-who-has-thus-attained"; a title of the Buddha by followers and also by himself.

Theravāda (P), Sthaviravāda (S): "The system or school of the Elders", considered to be the orthodox and original form of Buddhism as accepted and followed mainly in Ceylon, Burma, Thailand, Laos and Cambodia.

Three feelings: Pain, pleasure and freedom from both.

Three Jewels: Buddha, Dharma and Saṅgha. For monks and laymen initiation into Buddhism starts with a proclamation of allegiance, which runs like this:
        "I take my refuge in the Buddha.
        I take my refuge in the Dharma.
        I take my refuge in the Saṅgha."

T'ien-t'ai Tsung (Ch): The Chinese Buddhist school founded by Chih-i in the sixth century. It was also called the Fa-hua after the title of the text *Saddharma-puṇḍarīka* from which the doctrine of the school is derived.

Tīrthika: A heretic in India.

Tripiṭaka (S), Tipiṭaka (P): The Three Baskets:
    1. *Sūtra* (S), *Sutta* (P). Discourse, doctrine.

2. *Vinaya* (S & P). Rules of discipline.

3. *Abhidharma* (S), *Abhidhamma* (P). Discussion, metaphysics.

Twelve āyatanas (S & P): Twelve sense fields: eye, sight-objects, ear, sounds, nose, smells, tongue, tastes, body, touchable, mind and mind-objects.

Twelve Gate Treatise: See *Shih-erh-men-lun*.

Tzu-tsai-t'ien (Ch): See Īśvara.

Upaniṣads (S): A body of Hindu sacred literature that elaborates on the philosophical teachings of the Vedas.

Upāya (S & P): A device, convenient method, skillful or temporary means.

Vijñāna (S), Viññāna (P): Consciousness.

Vinaya (S & P): Rules of the Buddhist order; one of the three baskets of the Pali Canon.

Wei-sheng (Ch): That which is not yet produced or originated.

Wu (Ch): Nothing, non-being, inexistence.

Wu. (Ch): Thing.

Wu-pu-ch'ien (Ch): Things do not move.

Wu-hsin (Ch): No thought or mind.

Wu-wei (Ch): Non-action, passivity, action without action.

Wu-yin (Ch): Five *skandhas*, five aggregates.

Yin-yüan (Ch): Causes and conditions; causal conditions; causality.

Yogācāra (S & P): The Mind-Only School of Buddhism. It was founded by Asanga and Vasubandu in the fourth century. It is known as the Fa-hsiang School in China and the Hosso School in Japan.

Yu (Ch): Being, existence.

Yüan (Ch): Conditions or causal conditions.

Yüan (Ch): Source.

Yung (Ch): Function; activity; use.

Zen (Jap): The Japanese pronunciation of the Chinese ideograph for *ch'an*, which is derived from the Sanskrit *dhyāna*; the Chinese and Japanese Meditation School of Buddhism, established by Bodhidharma, the 28th Patriarch in India, who came to China around 520 A.D. as the First Patriarch in China.

LIST OF CHINESE TERMS

Ch'an 禪
Ch'an Tsung 禪宗
Ch'ang-an 長安
Chao-lun 肇論
chao-tz'u 造次
che-chung 折中
chen-k'ung wu-hsiang 眞空無相
cheng-chien 正見
chi-chia 即假
chi-chung 即中
chi-k'ung 即空
Chi-tsang 吉藏
chi-yen chi-hsing 奇言奇行
chia-hsiang 假相
Chia-hsiang Ta-shih 嘉祥大師
chia-ming 假名
ch'iang-ming-cheng 強名正
chiao-ti 教諦
chin-sheng 今生
ching 經
Ching-t'u Tsung 淨土宗
ch'ü-shih 去時
chu-shuo chung ti-i 諸說中第一
ch'üan 荃
Chuang-tzu 莊子
chüeh-tai-san-ti 絕待三諦
Chung-lun 中論
chung-tao 中道

erh-kuo 二過
erh-ti-san-kuan 二諦三觀

Fa-hsiang Tsung 法相宗
Fa-lang 法朗
Fa-tsang 法藏

fang-pien 方便
fei-yu fei-wu 非有非無
fen-pieh 分別

ho-luan 和鸞
hsi-lun 戲論
hsiang 相
hsing 生
hsing-hsiang 性相
hsing-yin 行陰
hsü 盡
Hsüan Tsang 玄奘
Hua-yen Tsung 華嚴宗
Hui-cheng-lun 廻諍論
hui-hui 恢恢
Hui-neng 慧能

i 羕
i-chia i-ch'ieh-chia 一假一切假
i-chih 一致
i-ch'u 己去
i-ch'u tse wu-erh 一處則無二
i-chung i-ch'ieh-chung 一中一切中
i-k'ung i-ch'ieh-k'ung 一空一切空
i-sheng 已生
i-yin 疑因

jan-jan-che 染染者
jen-sheng hsi-lun 人生戲論
Jih-chao 日照

k'o-hsiang 可相
k'o-p'o 可破
Kuan-shih-yin 觀世音
k'ung 空

lao 老
Lao-tzu 老子
li 理
liang-hsüan 兩玄
liu-ch'ing 六情
liu-chung 六種
Liu I-min 劉遺民

lun 論
Lung-shu 龍樹
Lung-shu-p'u-sa-chuan 龍樹菩隆傳

ming 名

nieh-p'an-wu-ming 涅槃無名

pa-pu-chung-tao 八不中道
Pai-lun 百論
pan-jo-wu-chih 般若無知
pen-sheng 本生
p'o-hsieh-hsien-cheng 破邪顯正
pu-chen-k'ung 不眞空

San-lun-hsüan-i 三論玄義
San-lun Tsung 三論宗
san-shih 三時
san-tsung-erh-ti 三種二諦
se-yin 色陰
Seng-chao 僧肇
Seng-ch'üan 僧詮
Seng-jui 僧叡
Seng-lang 僧朗
shan-mieh chu hsi-lun 善滅諸戲論
shen 神
shen-wo 神我
sheng 生
sheng-shr 生時
sheng-sheng 生生
shih 事
shih 實
shih 識
Shih-tsun 世尊
Shih-erh-men-lun 十二門論
Shih-erh-men-lun-chung-chih-i-chi 十二門論宗致義記
shih-hsiang 實相
shih-fang 十方
shou 受
ssu-chü 四句

t'a 他
Ta-ch'eng ta-i-chang 大乘大義章

Ta-chih-tu-lun 大智度論
T'ai-hsü 太虛
tao-ch'ang 道塲
Tao-te-ching 道德經
T'i-p'o 提婆
T'i-p'o-p'u-sa-chuan 提婆菩薩傳
t'ien 天
tien-p'ei 顛沛
T'ien-t'ai Tsung 天台宗
ting-hsing 定性
ting-yu 定有
tseng-shang-yüan 增上緣
tzu-hsing 自性
Tzu-tsai-t'ien 自在天
tz'u-ti-yüan 次第緣

wei-ch'ü 未去
wei-sheng 未生
wo 我
wu 無
wu 悟
wu 物
wu-lou 無漏
wu-hsin 無心
wu-pu-ch'ien 物不遷
wu-wei 無爲
wu-wu 無物
wu-yin 五陰
wu-yin 無因

yin-yüan 因緣
yu 有
yu-lou 有漏
yu-wei-fa 有爲法
yu-wu 有無
yu-wu hsiang-wei ku 有無相違故
yüan 緣
yüan 源
yüan-jung-san-ti 圓融三諦
yüan-yüan 緣緣
yung 用

SELECTED BIBLIOGRAPHY

Anchō: *Chūron shoki* 中論疏記 (A Commentary on the *Middle Treatise*), T 2255.

Āryadeva: *Kuang-pai-lun-pen* 廣百論本 (The Broad Hundred Treatise), T 1570.

————— : *Pai-lun* 百論 (The Hundred Treatise), T 1569.

————— : *Pai-tzu-lun* 百字論 (The Hundred Word Treatise), T 1572.

Baird, Robert D.: 'The Symbol of Emptiness and the Emptiness of Symbols', *Humanitas* 8 (1972), 221–242.

Bhattacharya, A. R.: '*Brahman* of Śankara and *Śūnyatā* of Mādhyamikas', *Indian Historical Quarterly* **XXXII** (1956), 270–285.

Bhattacharya, Kamaleswar: 'The Dialectical Method of Nāgārjuna', *Journal of Indian Philosophy* 1 (1971), 217–261.

Chan, Wing-tsit: *A Source Book in Chinese Philosophy* (Princeton University Press, Princeton, 1972).

Chang, Garma C. C.: *The Buddhist Teaching of Totality* (The Pennsylvania State University Press, University Park, 1974).

Chang, Man-tao (ed.): *San-lun-tien-chi-yen-chiu* 三論典籍研究 (Studies in San-lun Documents) (Ta-cheng-wen-hua Publishing Company, 1979).

————— : *San-lun-tsung-chih-fa-chan-chi-ch'i-szu-hsian* 三論宗之發展及其思想 (The Development of San-lun School and Its Thought) (Ta-cheng-wen-hua Publishing Company, 1978).

————— : *Chung-kuan-szu-hsian-lun-chi* 中觀思想論集 (The Collection of Essays on San-lun Thoughts) (Ta-cheng-wen-hua Publishing Company, 1978).

Chatterjee, Herampa Nath: *Mūla-Madhyamaka-Kārikā of Nāgārjuna* (Sanskrit College, Calcutta, 1957, Part I: Chapters I–V; 1962, Part II: Chapters VI–VII).

Ch'en, Kenneth: *Buddhism in China* (Princeton University Press, Princeton, 1964).

————— : 'Transformations in Buddhism in Tibet', *Philosophy East and West* **VII** (October, 1957; January, 1958).

Cheng, Hsueh-li: 'Nāgārjuna's Approach to the Problem of the Existence of God', *Religious Studies*, No. 12 (1976), 207–216.

————— : 'The Problem of God in Buddhism', *The Theosophist* **98** (1977), 98–108.

————— : 'Zen and San-lun Mādhyamika Thought: Exploring the Theoretical Foundation of Zen Teachings and Practices', *Religious Studies*, No. 15 (1979), 343–363.

————— : 'Nāgārjuna, Kant and Wittgenstein: The San-lun Mādhyamika Exposition of Emptiness', *Religious Studies*, No. 17 (1981), 67–85.

————— : 'Truth and Logic In San-lun Mādhyamika Buddhism', *International Philosophical Quarterly* **21** (1981).

————— : 'Chi-tsang's Treatment of Metaphysical Issues', *Journal of Chinese Philosophy* **8** (1981), 371–389.

Chi-tsang: *Chung-kuan-lun-su* 中觀論疏 (A Commentary on the *Middle Treatise*), T 1824.

————— : *Erh-ti-i* 二諦義 (The Meaning of Twofold Truth), T 1854.

————— : *Pai-lun-su* 百論疏 (A Commentary on the *Hundred Treatise*), T 1827.

————— : *San-lun-hsüan-i* 三論玄義 (The Profound Meaning of Three Treatises), T 1852.

————— : *Shih-erh-men-lun-su* 十二門論疏 (A Commentary on the *Twelve Gate Treatise*), T 1825.

Conze, Edward: *Buddhist Scriptures* (Penguin Books, Baltimore, 1966).

———— : *Buddhist Thought in India* (The University of Michigan Press, Ann Arbor, 1967).

———— : 'Meditations on Emptiness', *The Maha Bodhi* (1955), pp. 203– 211.

de Bary, William Theodore (ed.): *The Buddhist Tradition in India, China and Japan* (Modern Library, New York, 1969).

———— : *Sources of Indian Tradition*, 2 vols. (Columbia University Press, New York, 1958).

De Jong, Jan W.: *Cinq chapitres de la Prasannapadā* (Geuthner, Paris, 1949).

———— : 'Emptiness', *Journal of Indian Philosophy* **2** (1972), 7–15.

———— : 'The Problem of the Absolute in the Mādhyamika School', *Ibid.*, pp. 1–6.

Fa-tsang: *Shih-erh-men-lun tsung-chih-i-chi* 十二門論宗致義記 (Notations on the *Twelve Gate Treatise*), T 1826.

Fung, Yu-lan: *A History of Chinese Philosophy* (Derk Bodde, trans.), 2 vols (Princeton University Press, Princeton, 1953).

———— : *A Short History of Chinese Philosophy* (Derk Bodde, ed.). (The Free Press, New York, 1966).

Gard, Richard A.: 'On the Authenticity of the *Pai-lun* and *Shih-erh-men-lun*', *Indogaku Bukkyōgaku Kenkyū* **II** (1954), 751–742.

———— : 'On the Authenticity of the *Chung-lun*', *Ibid.* **III** (1954), 376– 370.

Hatani, Ryōtai: 'Dialectics of the Mādhyamika Philosophy', *Studies on Buddhism in Japan* (Tokyo, 1939), Vol. 1, pp. 53–71.

Huang, Ch'an-hua: *Chung-kuo fo-chiao-shih* 中國佛教史 (History of Chinese Buddhism) (Commercial Press, Shanghai, 1940).

Huang, Kung-wei: *Chung-kuo fo-chaio-ssu-hsiang-ch'uan-t'ung-shih* 中國佛教思想傳統史 (History of Chinese Buddhist Thought and Tradition) (Siao-lin. Taipei, 1972).

In-shun (Shih-in-shun): *Cheng-fo-chih-tao* 成佛之道 (The Way to Become Buddha) (Hui-jih Chiang-t'ang, Taipei, 1971).

————— : *Chung-kuan-chin-lun* 中觀今論 (The Contemporary Study of The Middle Way) (Hui-jih Chiang-t'ang, Taipei, 1971).

————— : *Chung-kuan-lun-song-chiang-chi* 中觀論頌講記 (An Exposition of the *Middle Treatise*) (Hui-jih Chiang-t'ang, Taipei, 1963).

————— : *Hsing-k'ung-hsüeh-t'an-yuan* 性空學探源 (Exploring the Source of the Emptiness of Essence) (Hui-jih Chiang-t'ang, Taipei, 1963).

Inada, Kenneth K.: *Nāgārjuna: A Translation of His Mūlamadhyamaka-kārikā with an Introductory Essay* (Hokuseido, Tokyo, 1970).

Kamata, Shigeo: 'Kūgan no chūgokuteki heni' 空觀の中國的變異 (Chinese Modification of *Śūnyatā-vāda*), *Indogaku Bukkyōgaku Kenkyū* **XVI** (1968), 522–527.

Karambelkar, V. W.: 'The Problem of Nāgārjuna', *Journal of Indian History* **XXX** (1952), 21–33.

Kumārajīva, *Lung-shu-p'u-sa-chuan* 龍樹菩薩傳 (Biography of Bodhisattva Nāgārjuna), T 2047.

————— : *T'i-p'o-p'u-sa-chuan* 提婆菩薩傳 (Biography of Bodhisattva Āryadeva), T 2048.

La Vallée Poussin, Louis de: *Mūlamadhyamakakārikās de Nāgārjuna avec la Prasannapadā de Candrakīrti* (*Bibliotheca Buddhica*, Vol. IV) (Imperial Academy of Sciences, St. Petersberg, 1913).

————— : 'Mādhyamaka', *Encyclopedia of Religion and Ethics*, James Hastings (ed.), Vol. VIII (T. & T. Clark, Edinburgh) (C. Scribner's Sons, New York, 1916).

————— : 'Notes on *Śūnyatā* and the Middle Path', *Indian Historical Quarterly*, No. 4 (1928), 161–168.

Lee, Shih-chieh: *San-lun-tsung-kang-yao* 三論宗綱要 (The Essentials of the San-lun School) (Hsieh-lin, Taipei, 1972).

Liebenthal, Walter: *The Book of Chao* (The Catholic University of Peking, Peking, 1948; Hong-kong University, Hong-kong, 1968).

Miyamoto, Shoson: 'The Buddha's First Sermon and Original Patterns of the Middle Way', *Indogaku Bukkyōgaku Kenkyū* **XIII** (1965), 855—845.

—————— : 'The Historical-social Bearings of the Middle Way', *Ibid.* **XIV** (1966), 996—969.

Murti, T. R. V.: *The Central Philosophy of Buddhism* (Allen and Unwin, London, 1955).

Nāgārjuna: *Chung-lun* 中論 (The Middle Treatise), T 1564.

—————— : *Hui-cheng-lun* 廻諍論 (The Refutation Treatise), T 1631.

—————— : *Shih-erh-men-lun* 十二門論 (The Twelve Gate Treatise), T 1568.

—————— : *Ta-ch'eng-p'o-yu-lun* 大乘破有論 (Refutation of the Concept of Being in the Mahāyāna), T 1574.

Nakamura, Hajime: 'Buddhist Logic Expounded by Means of Symbolic Logic', *Indogaku Bukkyōgaku Kenkyū* **VII** (1958), 395—375.

Narain, Harsh: '*Śūnyavāda*: A Reinterpretation', *Philosophy East and West* **XIII** (1964), 311—338.

Pandeya, R. C.: 'The Mādhyamika Philosophy: A New Approach', *Philosophy East and West* **XIV** (1964), 3—24.

Patkok, Sunitkumar: 'Life of Nāgārjuna', *Indian Historical Quarterly* **XXX** (1954), 93—95.

Ramanan, K. Venkata: 'A Fresh Appraisal of the Mādhyamika Philosophy', *Visvabharati Quarterly* **XXVII** (1961/62), pp. 230—238.

—————— : *Nāgārjuna's Philosophy as Presented in the Mahaprajñāpāramitā-Śāstra* (Bharatiya Vidya Prakashan, Varanasi, India, 1971).

Robinson, Richard H.: *Early Mādhyamika in India and China* (The University of Wisconsin Press, Madison, 1967).

—————— : 'Mysticism and Logic in Seng-chao's Thought', *Philosophy East and West* **VIII** (1958−59), 99−120.

—————— : 'Some Logical Aspects of Nāgārjuna's System', *Ibid.* **VI** (1957), 291−308.

Seng-chao: *Chao-lun* 肇論 (The Book of Chao), T 1858.

Silkstone, Thomas: 'My Self and My World', *International Philosophical Quarterly* **13** (1973), 377−390.

Sprung, Mervyn (ed.): *The Problem of Two Truths in Buddhism and Vedānta* (D. Reidel, Boston, 1973).

Stcherbatsky, Theodore: *Buddhist Logic*, 2 vols (Dover, New York, 1930).

—————— : *The Central Conception of Buddhism and the Meaning of the Word Dharma* (Susil Gupta, Ltd., Calcutta, 1956).

—————— : *The Conception of Buddhist Nirvāṇa* (Publishing Office of the Academy of Sciences of the U.S.S.R., Leningrad, 1927).

Streng, Frederick J.: 'The Buddhist Doctrine of Two Truths as Religious Philosophy', *Journal of Indian Philosophy* **1** (1971), 262−271.

—————— : *Emptiness: A Study in Religious Meaning* (Abingdon, New York, 1967).

—————— : 'Metaphysics, Negative Dialectic, and the Expression of the Inexpressible', *Philosophy East and West* **XXV** (1975), 429−447.

T'ai-hsü: *T'ai-hsü-ta-shih-ch'uan-shu* 太虛大師全書 (A Collection of Great Master T'ai-hsü's Writings), (Great Master T'ai-hsü Committee, Taipei, 1969), Vol. 13.

Taishō Shinshū Daizōkyō 大正新修大藏經 (Taishō Edition of the Chinese Tripiṭaka), Junjirō Takakusu and Kaikyoku Watanabe (eds.), 100 vols. (Daizō Shuppan Company, Tokyo, 1924−34).

Takakusu, Junjirō: *The Essentials of Buddhist Philosophy* (W. T. Chan and Charles A. Moore, eds.) (University of Hawaii, Honolulu, 1949).

T'ang, Yung-t'ung: *Han-wei Liang-chin Nan-pei-ch'ao Fo-chiao-shih* 漢魏兩晉南北朝佛教史 (History of Buddhism in Han, Wei, the Two Chins and Northern and Southern Dynasties) (Commercial Press, Shanghai, 1938).

Trundle Jr., Robert: 'Beyond the Linguistic and Conceptual: A Comparison of Albert Camus and Nāgārjuna', *Darshana International* XVI (1976), 1–11.

Tsukamoto, Zenryū (ed.): *Jōron Kenkyū* 肇論研究 (Studies in the Chao-lun) (Hōzonkan, Kyoto, 1960).

Tsunemoto, Kenyū: *Kūgan tetsugaku* 空觀哲學 (The Philosophy of Emptiness) (Daiichi Shobō, Tokyo, 1942).

Tucci, Giuseppe: *Pre-Diṅnāga Buddhist Texts on Logic from Chinese Sources* (Oriental Institute, Baroda, 1929).

——————— : 'Two Hymns of the *Catuḥ-stava* of Nāgārjuna', *Journal of Royal Asiatic Society* (1932), 309–325.

Ui, Hakuji: 'Sanron Kaidai' 三論解題 (The Explanation of Three Treatises), in *Kokuyaku Daizōkyō* (Kyusaka Tsuruda, ed.), Rombu V. (Kokumin Bunko Kankō-kai, Tokyo, 1921).

Vidyabhusana, S. C.: 'History of the Mādhyamika Philosophy of Nāgārjuna', *Journal of the Buddhist Text Society*, No. 4 (1897), 7–20.

——————— : 'The Mādhyamika School', *Ibid.*, No. 2 (1895), pp. 3–9, and No. 3, pp. 9–23.

Walleser, Max: 'The Life of Nāgārjuna from Tibetan and Chinese Sources', *Asia Major*, Hirth Anniversary Vol. (London, 1922), pp. 421–455.

Warren, Henry Clarke: *Buddhism in Translation* (Atheneum, New York, 1970).

Wayman, Alex: 'Contributions to the Mādhyamika School of Buddhism', *Journal of the American Oriental Society* 89, No. 1.

Zōkai: *Jūni monron sho monshi ki* 十二門論疏聞思記 (Notations on the Commentary of the Twelve Gate Treatise), T 2257.

INDEX OF NAMES

INDEX OF SUBJECTS

INDEX OF SUBJECTS
151

Ultimate, 14
Unreal, 16–18, 23, 51, 59–61, 66, 112
Unreality, 48
Upāya, 23, 106, 116

Validity, 20
Value, 14, 22, 24, 27, 41, 52
Vedanā, 57, 114
Vedānta, 37
Vehicle, 34, 54, 110–111
Verify, 68
Vidarba, 4
View, 8, 10–12, 17–18, 20–21, 23, 25–26, 32–33, 51, 63, 68–69, 82–83, 93, 96, 99–100, 108–109, 111
Vijñāna, 57, 114
Virtue, 11, 53, 111
Void, 9, 47
Vow, 4

Water, 24
Way, 11, 14–15, 18–19, 21, 25–26, 51–52, 79, 90, 93, 99, 108
West, 1
Wheel of existence, 53
Wheel of life and death, 31
Wisdom, 10, 14–15, 19–20, 22, 111, 116, 118
Woman, 21
Word, 19–24, 33–34, 112
World-honored, 94
Wrong, 21, 23
Wu, 16, 25

Yao, 14
Yin-yüan, 53
Yogacara, 6
Yu, 16, 25
Yukti-ṣaṣṭika, 5

Zen, 38